A Better Way

Paul's Guidebook for Church Unity

A Bible Study Workbook by Matthew Allen

© 2023 Spiritbuilding Publishers.

All rights reserved. No part of this book may be reproduced in any form without the written permission of the publisher.

Published by
Spiritbuilding Publishers
9700 Ferry Road, Waynesville, OH 45068

A BETTER WAY
Paul's Guidebook for Church Unity
By Matthew Allen

All Scripture references are taken from Holman Bible Publishers' Christian Standard Bible unless otherwise noted.

ISBN : 978-1955285-72-8

Spiritbuilding
PUBLISHERS

spiritbuilding.com

Table of Contents

	Why This Study?	1
Lesson 1	Congregational Oneness	3
Lesson 2	For the Common Good	11
Lesson 3	Unity and Diversity	19
Lesson 4	God Put the Body Together	26
Lesson 5	If I Don't Have Love	33
Lesson 6	Love Is	40
Lesson 7	Love Never Ends	48
Lesson 8	Welcome Each Other	53
Lesson 9	Build Up One Another	61
Lesson 10	Please and Rejoice with One Another	71
Lesson 11	Keeping the Unity of the Spirit	81
Lesson 12	What Makes Us One?	87
Lesson 13	Standing Firm in One Spirit	94
	Endnotes	102

Why This Study?

As I write it feels as if there is a certain angst about the future in our nation. Every day the news is filled with troubling headlines. We see the vicious political and social rhetoric fueled by biased media who care only about the number of clicks generated and ad revenue produced. The cultural and political divide is hardening. More than ever, people in our country view those who disagree with them on politics, social matters, and religion as a threat to the country. We see it every day as millions of people parrot their favorite talking points through social media. Those who disagree with them are seen as an enemy. Millions more have simply shut down. They simply can't handle it. The stress and anxiety are too much. Others simply do not want to endure the cascade of negativity and bile that will be spewed upon them if they do speak out. It is less stressful to simply withdraw and stay away from the fray.

This is all the work of Satan who thrives on division. He lives for destruction of every good thing. Jesus identified him as the father of lies, John 8.44. In the garden, his false and misleading statements drove a wedge between Eve and God. The rest as they say is history. *Every division begins with a lie.* As we examine the story in Genesis 3.1–5, we easily see how Satan got a foothold by planting seeds of doubt and distrust. After Eve and Adam believed Satan's deception, our world has never been the same.

Inside our nation, the enemy's work is alive and well. He is systematically dividing our nation ... perhaps like never before. America may well be lost without a shot fired. It is likely to be destroyed from within because its most basic institutions will implode by the endless pursuit of self. Satan's work seems to be thriving inside every facet of society. By way of division, he is separating us individually from God, ripping our families apart, dividing our communities, and fomenting cynicism toward our governing and educational institutions.

Focusing on the family, think of what the destructiveness of secular humanism has done inside the home over the last 80 years. God and respect for His principles have been completely removed. We see fatherless homes, the endless cycle of teen pregnancy, relentless materialism and debt, the profligacy of sexual immorality, and easy divorce. At least two generations have grown up with trust issues so significant that they fear the commitment of marriage and simply live together all the while having a quick exit strategy if things don't work out. The birthrate in our nation has reached historic lows. The lack of family stability is crippling our nation.

Weak families make weak churches.

The same issues impacting our families are bearing themselves out in the church ... much of it driven by selfish individualism characterized by an exaggerated view of one's opinions, a disregard for the hearts and feelings of others, and the ignoring of basic biblical principles on managing relationships. When disagreements happen some simply do not know how to handle it. A person can go from calm to the height of anger over the simplest things, often without warning. Too often we see a lack of self-control, the judging of motives, and a lack of patience with others. When these things are absent in our personal life, it impacts the local church.

There needs to be more teaching on the basic matters of love for brethren, respect for leadership and one another, patience, and dependence upon God. We need a greater understanding of the gift of unity and how to maintain it. Teaching on unity also brings the need to instill courage, because when we practice it, Satan will attack. This is the aim behind this workbook.

As we go through our study, we will examine much of Paul's writing to the church in Corinth. Paul spent 18 months at this church teaching and encouraging it. After his departure he received reports of problems. Division, carnality, jealousy, agendas, and confusion over spiritual gifts had this congregation on the verge of upheaval. In his writing, Paul urges them:

- To be one and speak the same thing.
- To come to a proper understanding of the source and purpose of spiritual gifts.
- To develop an appreciation for others within the body and appreciate the diverse set of talents and abilities God had blessed them with.
- To do everything out of love and consideration for each other.
- To place a priority on edification and building up of one another.

We will also examine Paul's writing to the Roman, Ephesian and Philippian churches, where he stressed that we have the right attitude toward unity and work to maintain what God has given us. These are principles that must not be ignored. May we all heighten our awareness of them and resolve to live according to Jesus' prayer in John 17:20–21:

> "I pray not only for these, but also for those who believe in me through their word. [21] May they all be one, as you, Father, are in me and I am in you. May they also be in us, so that the world may believe you sent me.

Thanks for being a part of this study.

Matthew Allen

July 2023

Lesson 1

Congregational Oneness
1 Corinthians 1.10–17
Overview

If you have ever been through a church split, as I have, you know the lasting pain and brokenness that comes to individuals, families, and their children. I was 11 years old when it happened, and I've never forgotten what my parents and grandparents went through as they were part of the group who had to leave and completely start over forming a new congregation. Those who stayed at the old congregation were never the same … and within ten years that local church folded. Division, cliques, and factionalism can break up the strongest churches. It remains a prevalent problem. Churches today still get divided over what some have called "theological trivia," personality preferences, and political and social agendas.

All these differences lead to jealousy and quarreling. Much of it stems from allowing the attitudes of the world to creep back in where they should not be. Vanity and self-will are almost always the causes of divisions and factions inside a congregation.

The Bigger Picture

During the time of the Roman Empire the church met mainly in homes. Typically, these were the homes of wealthy Christians, whose homes could hold larger numbers of people. The church at Corinth may have consisted of a few house churches … creating an atmosphere conducive for division. Coupled with this were the sharp differences in social class, economic position, and cultural background. All of these things led to significant problems within the Corinthian church. Paul writes the first letter to answer a series of questions he received and to set straight the things that had gotten into disorder.

The Text

NLT:

1 Corinthians 1:10–17

[10] I appeal to you, dear brothers and sisters, by the authority of our Lord Jesus Christ, to live in harmony with each other. Let there be no divisions in the church. Rather, be of one mind, united in thought and purpose. [11] For some members of Chloe's household have told me about your quarrels, my dear brothers and sisters. [12] Some of you are saying, "I am a follower of Paul." Others are saying, "I follow Apollos," or "I follow Peter," or "I follow only Christ." [13] Has Christ been divided into factions? Was I, Paul, crucified for you? Were any of you baptized in the name of Paul? Of course not! [14] I thank God that I did not baptize any of you except Crispus and Gaius, [15] for now no one can say they were baptized in my name. [16] (Oh yes, I also baptized the household of Stephanas, but I don't remember baptizing anyone else.) [17] For Christ didn't send me to baptize, but to preach the Good News—and not with clever speech, for fear that the cross of Christ would lose its power.

CSB:

1 Corinthians 1:10–17

[10] Now I urge you, brothers and sisters, in the name of our Lord Jesus Christ, that all of you agree in what you say, that there be no divisions among you, and that you be united with the same understanding and the same conviction. [11] For it has been reported to me about you, my brothers and sisters, by members of Chloe's people, that there is rivalry among you. [12] What I am saying is this: One of you says, "I belong to Paul," or "I belong to Apollos," or "I belong to Cephas," or "I belong to Christ." [13] Is Christ divided? Was Paul crucified for you? Or were you baptized in Paul's name? [14] I thank God that I baptized none of you except Crispus and Gaius, [15] so that no one can say you were baptized in my name. [16] I did, in fact, baptize the household of Stephanas; beyond that, I don't recall if I baptized anyone else. [17] For Christ did not send me to baptize, but to preach the gospel—not with eloquent wisdom, so that the cross of Christ will not be emptied of its effect.

Explore the Text

1. When beginning to correct the Corinthians on their bickering and quarreling, why do you think Paul invoked the name of Christ? How does Christ bind us together?

2. In the local church, why should divisiveness be strongly resisted?

3. What does it mean to you to be *united with the same understanding*?

4. What type of attitude toward unity must we possess? (Paul says we are to be *united with the same conviction*).

5. What does a party spirit lead to? (1.12)

6. What is the governing principle found in 1.13?

7. What is the priority Paul outlines in 1.14–17?

About the Text

1 Corinthians 1.10 easily serves as the thesis statement for the entire letter. It is as if Paul is coming alongside them and urging them with all his apostolic authority to respond in a positive manner to what Christ has done for them. The tone is corrective in nature. The focus is on the local church. The matter is serious. Each one of them belong to Christ. Each of them should regard each other as brethren and move in harmony with each other. Because they were one in fellowship with Christ, they should be one in fellowship with each other.

I. **1.10: Be one in fellowship with each other.**
    A. *Agree in what you say.*
      i. This phrase was a popular figure of speech from Greek political life that urged the dropping of the party spirit.[1] This admonition is positive.
      ii. The emphasis was to be on the centrality of Christ and the fundamental nature of the gospel.
      iii. This is seen as we examine 1.18—3.23.
          1. They were to unite around the message or *word of the cross*, see 1.18.
          2. It is also referred to as a message of *wisdom* in 2.6.
          3. The *word of the cross* is nothing more than apostolic doctrine, which serves as the standard we must live by.
      iv. *Keep living by that same standard to which we have attained,* Philippians 3.16 NASB.
    B. *Let there be no divisions among you.*
      i. *Divisions* in 1.10 comes from the word we use today for "schism." The word carries the imagery of tearing or ripping apart, i.e., the "plowing" of a field.
          1. The same word is used in John's gospel (7.40–43; 9.16; 10.19–21) to describe those who were arguing amongst themselves over their impressions of Jesus, i.e., who He was and what His mission was.
          2. Schisms in the church often revolve around differences in judgment and lead to dissension. Those who cause such things are to be avoided, Romans 16.17.
      ii. In the case of the Corinthians, differing groups in the local church held differing opinions about various church leaders, which was leading to jealousy and quarrels. Cliques had formed and were competing against each other.
    C. *Be united with the same understanding and the same conviction.*
      i. *United* comes from the word we use for being "knit together."

            1. This word is also found in Mark 1.19 where we read of the "mending or restoring" of fishing nets, bones, or torn garments.
            2. The NASB 2020 translates the word as being *made complete*. The basic idea is to put back together. Grow together.
        ii. We are to be united in our beliefs, standards, and attitudes toward spiritual life.
II. **1.11–12: Misplaced Identity**
    A. Members of the Corinthian church were rallying around their preferred church leaders and disregarding or rejecting others.
        i. This was quite common in Greco-Roman culture in how ancient political parties were formed. Differing groups would assemble, disagreements would ensue, with each shouting over the other, often with hatred and abuse. This all too familiar practice appears to have been creeping into the Corinthian church.
        ii. At Corinth, the party spirit was probably being fueled by the cultural differences between Jew and Gentile, 2 Corinthians 11.13. Jews were probably claiming to be of the party of Peter, while Gentiles probably identified more with Paul. Some of these parties may have aligned themselves with culture and quality of preaching, of which Apollos would be in view.
    B. The main problem Paul is addressing is the focus on self and the usage of the word "I". Below all the quarreling and wrangling was a self-centered, self-willing exclusiveness that is the opposite of unity and harmony.
III. **1.13a: Christ is Not Divided**
    A. *Is Christ divided?* The answer is obvious. Christ is not divided.
        i. He died to bring us together, Ephesians 2.13–16.
        ii. He died so that *there would be no division in the body, but that the members would have the same concern for each other*, 1 Corinthians 12.25.
    B. A divided church contradicts Paul's teaching in 1 Corinthians 12.12–13 and Romans 12.5.
    C. The church is one with the Father, Son, and the Spirit.
IV. **1.13b–17: What Matters is the Mission**
    A. 1.13b—Paul was not happy that some were claiming allegiance to him over Christ. The only allegiance a Christian has is to Christ.
    B. 1.14–16—Paul was unsure of the exact number he had baptized at Corinth. Numbers weren't important to him.

What was important was that souls were being saved.
- C. 1.17—His mission (and ours) is to preach the gospel ... the message of the cross ... with converts coming to a oneness with Christ ... not to build factions around prominent teachers and preachers.

Reaction

1. Why is a unified message around the centrality of Christ and the fundamental aspects of the gospel so important?

2. Why are cliques so detrimental to the life of the local church? What can we do to make sure they do not form?

3. The emphasis in the last part of v. 10 is for the Corinthian church to reject cliques and *grow back together*. As we think about our own diverse group of Christians here, what type of things can we do to facilitate the process of growing together?

4. What types of attitudes fuel divisiveness? What must we do to eliminate these things from our lives?

5. Do we have any loyalties to preachers, institutions, and parties in today's church? While we all may have differing preferences, styles, and approaches, what can we do individually to make sure these do not become sources of division and strife?

6. Why is focusing on the mission of such great importance? What will happen to all the "side issues" as we concentrate on getting out the message of the cross?

For the Christian Today

Unity for His people has always been God's desire. *How delightfully good when brothers live together in harmony,* Psalm 133.1. And who could forget Paul's writing in Romans 15.5–7:

> Now may the God who gives endurance and encouragement grant you to live in harmony with one another, according to Christ Jesus, so that you may glorify the God and Father of our Lord Jesus Christ with one mind and one voice. Therefore welcome one another, just as Christ also welcomed you, to the glory of God.

God wants us to be one in mind, love, spirit or attitude, and purpose, Philippians 2.2. He is the source of our unity. We have been called to maintain it and guard against destroying it. We do so by moving with a spirit of humility and considering the needs of others above ourselves, Philippians 2.3–4. We maintain unity by refusing to insist on our own way, determining not to get into squabbles or bicker, and by focusing on the mission our Lord has given to us and His people.

This is for the glory of God. Unity reflects who He is. It displays His amazing power of grace, mercy, and forgiveness to a dying world. Just as Christ has accepted us for the glory of God, so we are to accept one another to His glory.

Unity must be genuine. Our attitude toward unity should always be sincere. We are not simply *pretending to agree* while stubbornly holding on to our disagreements and objections. Such attitudes limit our productiveness within the congregation and almost always impact our happiness as well as the happiness of others.

Unity does not demand uniformity. A football team whose players all wanted to play quarterback would have uniformity but not unity. It would be impossible for it to function as a team if everyone played the same position. When Paul communicates the need to agree and hold to the same convictions he does not rule out our own individual uniqueness and perspective. This is clearly seen later in 1 Corinthians, specifically chapter 12. We are all different from each other in personality, talents, and temper.

Despite this, the expectation is for us to be of one mind. When differences arise, the priority is to work them out.

Pray For ...

1. Help in examining your heart and actions, setting aside self-centeredness and ego-driven motivations, focusing on pleasing others for their good and spiritual development.
2. Unity within your local church family and the brotherhood, mending divisions and cultivating harmony, understanding, and shared convictions among believers.
3. A deeper understanding of the significance of the sacrifice of Christ and the unifying power He brings. Pray that your priorities will align with His mission, freeing you from divisive attitudes so that you can focus on preaching the gospel and bringing souls to oneness with Him.

Journal

What are some things you can do personally to avoid quarreling and squabbling with brothers and sisters within the congregation? How can you promote congregational oneness?

For Further Reading

Read through the following passages in the New Testament that stress unity with Christ and unity with each other: John 15.1–7; John 17.20–23; Galatians 3.26–29; Philippians 2.1–4. What are some principles you see from these passages?

Lesson 2

For the Common Good

1 Corinthians 12.1–11

Overview

1 Corinthians 12 begins a major section inside the book. It focuses on spiritual gifts, of which every member of the church has been given. These are the way that God uses us to proclaim His word to the world and minister to others inside and outside the church. Each gift is a tool God has given that we can use to grow, worship, testify, and serve. Spiritual gifts are also a powerful testimony of God's power to bring people together in oneness, harmony, and power. God's gifts have been given to build up the church.

The Bigger Picture

Supernatural spiritual gifts had been given by the Spirit to the Corinthians. They came to regard the possession of these gifts as a matter of pride and were setting believers against each other based on who possessed what gift. The more visible and public the gift, the more important a person was viewed. By doing so, they created division and subverted the purpose for which they were given. The Spirit gave gifts for the common benefit of all and for the unity of the local church. In the local church, there is no A-Team or B-Team … members are all one. The main idea presented in these verses is that there is great diversity in the gifts that have been received that all originate from a single, unified source.

The Text

NLT:

1 Corinthians 12:1–11

[1] Now, dear brothers and sisters, regarding your question about the special abilities the Spirit gives us. I don't want you to misunderstand this. [2] You know that when you were still pagans, you were led astray and swept along in worshiping speechless idols. [3] So I want you to know that no one speaking by the Spirit of God will curse Jesus, and no one can say Jesus is Lord, except by the Holy Spirit. [4] There are different kinds of spiritual gifts, but the same Spirit is the source of them all. [5] There are different kinds of service, but we serve the same Lord. [6] God works in different ways, but it is the same God

who does the work in all of us. [7] A spiritual gift is given to each of us so we can help each other. [8] To one person the Spirit gives the ability to give wise advice; to another the same Spirit gives a message of special knowledge. [9] The same Spirit gives great faith to another, and to someone else the one Spirit gives the gift of healing. [10] He gives one person the power to perform miracles, and another the ability to prophesy. He gives someone else the ability to discern whether a message is from the Spirit of God or from another spirit. Still another person is given the ability to speak in unknown languages, while another is given the ability to interpret what is being said. [11] It is the one and only Spirit who distributes all these gifts. He alone decides which gift each person should have.

CSB:

1 Corinthians 12:1–11

[1] Now concerning spiritual gifts: brothers and sisters, I do not want you to be unaware. [2] You know that when you were pagans, you used to be enticed and led astray by mute idols. [3] Therefore I want you to know that no one speaking by the Spirit of God says, "Jesus is cursed," and no one can say, "Jesus is Lord," except by the Holy Spirit. [4] Now there are different gifts, but the same Spirit. [5] There are different ministries, but the same Lord. [6] And there are different activities, but the same God works all of them in each person. [7] A manifestation of the Spirit is given to each person for the common good: [8] to one is given a message of wisdom through the Spirit, to another, a message of knowledge by the same Spirit, [9] to another, faith by the same Spirit, to another, gifts of healing by the one Spirit, [10] to another, the performing of miracles, to another, prophecy, to another, distinguishing between spirits, to another, different kinds of tongues, to another, interpretation of tongues. [11] One and the same Spirit is active in all these, distributing to each person as he wills.

Explore the Text

1. What are we saying when we say, "Jesus is Lord"? What does the term "Lord" mean?

2. What are the "gifts" Paul is referring to in 12.4?

3. How is diversity inherent in unity?

4. What is the purpose of receiving spiritual gifts?

5. Who is the source of our spiritual gifts?

6. How many people received spiritual gifts? See 12.6. Why would this be important to consider?

7. What do you think is the meaning of *the common good* in 12.7?

8. How many times in 12.1–11 does Paul mention that gifts are given by the Spirit? Why would he concentrate on this so much?

About the Text

Every member of the church has been given gifts by God which are to be used in ministering to others and sharing the gospel. It appears that the Corinthian Christians were tending to exalt one or a few gifts over the others. Some viewed tongue speaking as great while at the same time denigrating other gifts. Therefore, they were turning these blessings from God into something He never intended: sources of cliques and personal glory. In this chapter Paul will explain the origin and purpose of the gifts they received, as well as how to distinguish between those who made legitimate claims to them and those who did not.

I. **12.1–3—How to Examine the Authenticity of Spiritual Gifts**
   A. *I do not want you to be unaware.*
  i. Paul wanted to correct them on their understanding of the things of the Spirit.
    B. Paul reminds them of their pagan past. At that time many of them had been influenced by and led to false gods. Like Christians, pagans had spiritual experiences as well, but they were to be rejected because the practices came from idol worship.
    C. Believers who confess Jesus as the Son of God and Lord of their life will speak and act in ways that glorify Jesus. This is the result of the work of the Spirit.
  i. No true believer is going to claim that "Jesus is cursed."

II. **12.4–7—Unity in Diversity**
   A. 12.4: The Spirit distributes gifts in many different forms or varieties. They can be speaking gifts or serving gifts (1 Peter 4.11).
  i. Just as the *one* Spirit, Lord, and God manifest themselves in a variety of ways and ministries, so the Spirit has equipped members of the church to work in a variety of ways and ministries.
  ii. The unity of God does not imply unity of gifts.
  iii. Rather, the one and same God is responsible for the variety itself.

B. 12.5: The gifts are given so they might be used as tools in ministry. They are to be used in service in the name of the Lord.
    i. These ministries are varied. Some are gifted to teach children. Others are gifted public speakers, while others work closely with people in one-on-one situations. Some are good at emphasizing doctrine, others are great in giving mercy and comfort, etc. The specialties are endless because the emphasis is on variety.
    ii. The gifts are not given for self-edification or self-service. They are not for us but for others. See 1 Peter 4.10.
  C. 12.6: The gifts we receive are worked out by the power of God.
    i. "Activities" in this verse means "effect" or "results."
    ii. The exercising of our gifts is not for our personal prestige or acclaim. God is the one who empowers us.
  D. 12.7: Gifts have been given to bring us together. The objective is *for the common good.*
    i. They are intended to help, bring a benefit, or to be advantageous to other believers who God has brought together in His name.
    ii. By exercising our gifts, we also help others discover and use their own gifts more effectively.

III. **12.8–11—Varieties of Spiritual Gifts**
  A. 12.8–10: These verses illustrate the varieties of gifts mentioned in 12.4.
    i. Some of the gifts were temporary. Others were permanent.
    ii. This is not an exhaustive list of spiritual gifts. Other lists are found in 1 Corinthians 12.28; Romans 12.6–8; and 1 Peter 4.11.
  B. 12.11: The common source of the gifts is the Spirit.

Reaction

1. Do you think the "gifts" in view here are supernatural, natural, or both? Explain.

2. Does the Spirit give us gifts today? Who all receives the gifts? (Ephesians 4.7)

3. What is the expectation that comes with the receiving of a gift?

4. Why is it important that we appreciate and value the variety of gifts God has given?

5. What are some examples of the variety of ministries God has given us inside our local church?

6. By whose power are these gifts being employed? Who gets the glory?

7. For what purpose have these things been given (12.7) and who is the source (12.11)?

For the Christian Today

Unity in diversity is a good thing. Your favorite football team would wind up last in the conference each year if all 11 players came out as quarterbacks … no matter if they were each the best in the country. In fact, they would probably not even score a single point all year. A successful team will effectively use every part it has to accomplish what is good and achieve victory. As we look inside the body of the local church, we need to value every member. They all have a role on the team and a purpose to fulfill. Different backgrounds, experiences, education, talents, and perspectives are all part of what makes the local body function. Each one needs to appreciate the diversity God has blessed us with. With it, we can reach far more people than we would otherwise.

We must use our gift. Everyone has received a gift, Ephesians 4.7. On your last birthday or Christmas, you may have received a gift from someone that you did not use. It may be tucked away in a drawer somewhere. Don't treat the gift you have received from God like that. Your gift is a reflection of God's love. What does it say if you disregard it? *Just as each one has received a gift, use it to serve others, as good stewards of the varied grace of God,* 1 Peter 4.10. We are stewards of God's gifts. He intends to use those gifts for the benefit of others. It was never in God's vision that we have a professional class inside the church where a few especially talented people carry on the work while everyone else sits back and watches. Everyone has a gift, and everyone is expected to use it.

The exercising of your gift encourages others to use their gift. Here we bring in the Hebrew writer's familiar words: *let us consider one another in order to provoke love and good works,* Hebrews 10.24. Our gifts were never intended to be only for us or for our glory. They have been given *for the common good,* 1 Corinthians 12.7. The Christian who ministers to others with his gift of service, encourages others to serve. For example, one who exercises his gift of mercy and compassion inspires the other members of the body to be filled with mercy and compassion. If this is true, then so is the opposite. If we fail in the exercising of our gift, we become a hindrance to others in the exercising of their gift.

When the church works together exercising its variety of gifts amazing things happen. Every member in the local church will begin to experience the byproduct of their service by being blessed by God and by others. The local church will have a powerful testimony inside its community … demonstrating the transforming energy of the gospel before unbelievers. Leaders will also become apparent, which is essential for the local church to function properly. And finally, the congregation will experience great joy in abiding unity, love, and fellowship. This is the *maintaining unity in the bond of peace,* Ephesians 4.3, that Paul had in mind. This result is not produced by us … it is a byproduct of the work of the Spirit who dwells inside.

Pray For …

1. God to reveal any misconceptions or imbalances in your understanding and usage of the gifts and abilities He has given you, granting you the perspective to use them for the common good and the advancement of His kingdom.

2. Humility and selflessness as you work in the local church, utilizing your gifts and abilities for the benefit and edification of others, building unity and mutual growth within the church.

3. The desire to do everything for the glory of God.

Journal

As you think about the gift God has given you, what are some things you can do to use it more effectively in the kingdom? How will the exercising of it help others? How will it encourage them to use their gift? What are some things you can do this week to put this into practice?

For Further Reading

Read through Romans 12.1–8 and 1 Corinthians 12.28. What are some of the types of gifts listed here? What are some of the attitudes Paul speaks of that we must keep in mind as we use our gifts?

Lesson 3

Unity and Diversity

1 Corinthians 12.12–20

Overview

Previously we discussed how unity and diversity is a good thing. The body of Christ would not function without it. We also talked about how we are stewards of the gift(s) God has given us and are expected to put them to use in the kingdom. As we work, we will be an encouragement to others to exercise their gift. And finally, we talked about when each member is doing their part amazing things happen inside the church, where it is led toward maturity and the gospel message is spread. In this lesson we will see how Paul expands on his discussion of unity and diversity. The church is like a body, with each member sharing a common origin through their regeneration which occurred at baptism. In that moment each believer is drenched in the Spirit and brought together as one into the body of the saints. Because we share the same origin, there is no room for pride or arrogance. In fact, every member is dependent upon the other. God has arranged the parts inside the body just as He wills.

The Bigger Picture

The Corinthian church had come to look a lot like the world. They had essentially brought in the culture of their day into the life of the church (hierarchy, classism, sexually immoral behavior, etc.). Paul's goal in this chapter deals with their tendency to want to divide up into classes or divisions over the type of spiritual gifts members received. Those who had the more public gifts were seen as more important as those who did not. And those with the public gifts were lording it over others … that their gift made them more spiritual than the "quiet" gifts. Paul needed to get them to understand that every person is important inside the body and has a place where they can influence others.

The Text

NLT:

1 Corinthians 12:12–20

[12] The human body has many parts, but the many parts make up one whole body. So it is with the body of Christ. [13] Some of us are Jews, some are Gentiles, some are slaves, and some are free. But we have all been baptized into one body by one Spirit, and we all share the same Spirit. [14] Yes, the body has many different parts, not just one part. [15] If the foot says, "I am not a part of the body because I am not a hand," that does not make it any less a part of the body. [16] And if the ear says, "I am not part of the body because I am not an eye," would that make it any less a part of the body? [17] If the whole body were an eye, how would you hear? Or if your whole body were an ear, how would you smell anything? [18] But our bodies have many parts, and God has put each part just where he wants it. [19] How strange a body would be if it had only one part! [20] Yes, there are many parts, but only one body.

CSB:

1 Corinthians 12:12–20

[12] For just as the body is one and has many parts, and all the parts of that body, though many, are one body—so also is Christ. [13] For we were all baptized by one Spirit into one body—whether Jews or Greeks, whether slaves or free—and we were all given one Spirit to drink. [14] Indeed, the body is not one part but many. [15] If the foot should say, "Because I'm not a hand, I don't belong to the body," it is not for that reason any less a part of the body. [16] And if the ear should say, "Because I'm not an eye, I don't belong to the body," it is not for that reason any less a part of the body. [17] If the whole body were an eye, where would the hearing be? If the whole body were an ear, where would the sense of smell be? [18] But as it is, God has arranged each one of the parts in the body just as he wanted. [19] And if they were all the same part, where would the body be? [20] As it is, there are many parts, but one body.

Explore the Text

1. Why do you think Paul was being so adamant regarding diversity in the body? Why the need to remind them of the diversity of parts?

2. What or who made the Corinthians one? When did this happen? (12.13)

3. How does Paul illustrate the point of 12.14? (See 12.15–17)

4. Who arranged the members of the body? Why is that important to understand?

5. What impact would the body make if it were all the same part?

About the Text

In this section, Paul begins to illustrate the oneness of the church itself. What makes it one? It is the diversity of the many parts working together in unison. Diversity is a key element of God's plan, demonstrating His power and grace. But each member also needs to recognize and accept his part or place inside the body. If he or she does not, it will become a source of division and bring discord.

I. 12.12–13—**Unity and Its Origin**
    A. 12.12: The human body is a perfect example to illustrate the unity and interconnectedness of the church.
      i. Just as the human body is one with many differing parts (members) so is the body of Christ.
      ii. Each member has its own gift and function but works for the common good of the whole.
      iii. The variety of differing parts must not cancel out unity … instead it should be worked out in the daily life of the church.
    B. 12.13: The source of our unity is the Spirit.
      i. Upon the occasion of our baptism, we were regenerated by the Spirit, bringing us from spiritual death into life, and placed into the body of Christ. *Every Christian has been baptized in the Spirit.*
      ii. Drinking of the Spirit does not refer to communion. Rather, the Spirit has been given in overflowing abundance to every believer in the church. As one writer says, we *have been drenched in the Spirit.*
      iii. We share a common bond in the body because everyone of us has been plunged into and drenched with the Spirit.[2]
    C. Since the gifts come from the Spirit and are assigned/arranged by the Father (12.18), there is no basis for pride or arrogance. The gifts we have do not represent our personal spirituality or excellence. Rather, they have been given for the good of the local church.

II. 12.14–16: **The Unity and Diversity of the Body**
    A. The church is like a body. Our bodies are characterized by unity and diversity. The fact that diversity exists is not a threat to unity. In fact, it is an essential to the functioning and effectiveness of the body.
    B. Every part is vital. No person is inferior, inconsequential, or unnecessary. Every member is needed for the body to function.

III. **12.17–20: God Places the Parts of the Body Where He Wills**
    A. Self-promotion kills the spirit of unity. This is why Paul wrote not *to think of (yourself) more highly than (you) should think. Instead, think sensibly, as God has distributed a measure of faith to each one*, Romans 12.3.
      i. Looking down or excluding other members, disparaging their gifts, harms the body. One writer refers to it as "self-mutilation".
    B. God has placed every individual in the body exactly where He wants them to be. The gifts reflect His oversight and wisdom. From the beginning, God has designed His church to have many parts, but be one body.

Reaction

1. In your mind, what should the church look like as it works out its diversity of gifts in the every day life of the church? Explain.

2. Why do you think Paul continues to remind his readers (and us) that our gifts are gifts from the Spirit? Why is understanding their origin so vital to unity in the church?

3. Verses 14–16 describe our interconnectedness and dependence upon other members of the local church for proper functioning. Can we effectively carry out our spiritual responsibilities if we do not have a strong connection (relationship) with the other members?

4. Does diversity threaten unity, or is it vital to it? Explain.

5. Is there any part of the spiritual body that is inconsequential or unnecessary? What can you do to encourage fellow members from feeling that way? How does this fit into the charge to *build up the body,* 14.26b.

6. How does self-promotion kill unity?

7. How does an understanding that God has placed you in the body exactly where He wants you help as you think about your role in the church?

For the Christian Today

Every part is designed to work. In his illustration, Paul used the senses of touch, sight, smell, and hearing. Without those, we are limited. (I don't think I ever appreciated my sense of smell more than after it came back from battling COVID-19.) We need to be thankful that there are those who add what we cannot. Together, we work. Together, we get things done. Ephesians 4.16 presents us with some great thoughts on how everyone works. *Every joint supplies,* Paul says. Problems arise when some don't supply. They just take. Like a hitchhiker who hopes you'll stop and pick them up and carry them to their destination, they are just along for the ride and don't help in any way. When the church has taken them as far as they want to go, they'll get out. We all need to be adding and supplying to the whole. Encouragement and prayers are the easiest way we can help. Its serving as shepherds and deacons. Its teaching classes. Its giving up a Saturday for someone who needs help. Its staying late after services to talk to someone who is discouraged. Supplying. Adding. Doing our part. Working. *Every joint supplies.*[3]

Interdependence is something to be valued. Most of us seem to prefer *independence.* Culture has ingrained us not to want to need other people. Dependence is often associated with weakness or deficiency.[4] People of our age take pride in their autonomy. Whether we realize this or not, our cultural bent can play a role into how unity is worked out in the day-to-day life of the church. God has designed church life to be enhanced by interdependence, where each member can be harmoniously dependent upon others for his or her identity.

The church functions as a body. The church is not a collection of separate individuals going around doing their own thing. The church is not a democracy. The church does not divide itself into partisan groups (1 Corinthians 1.13). Every part is vitally connected and is to function like a body. If a member is not doing his or her job, then someone else must do the work for which they are not equipped. The only way the church can function as it should is by each person using the gift the Spirit has given them just as God desired. We all have what God desires for us. *Think sensibly, as God has distributed a measure of faith to each one,* Romans 12.3b. We should each receive our gift with profound thanks. We should see the usage of that gift as a privilege.

Pray For ...

1. A deeper understanding and appreciation of the diverse gifts/talents and functions within the body of Christ, helping you embrace the unique contributions of every member for the effective functioning of the church.

2. Humility in your heart regarding your gifts and the gifts of others, and that you be guarded against pride, comparison, or self-promotion, so that you may nurture a spirit of gratitude, contentment, and collaboration within the body of Christ.

3. Alignment with where God has placed you within the body, surrendering your desires and preferences, faithfully fulfilling your role, and recognizing that your contribution is part of God's greater work in the church.

Journal

What are some things you can do to develop a stronger connection with other members of the local body? What is your plan this week to put this into action?

For Further Study

Today's passage in 1 Corinthians 12 parallels Paul's teaching in Ephesians 4.11–16. How are these passages similar? What can we learn when we tie them together?

Lesson 4

God Put the Body Together

1 Corinthians 12.21–30

Overview

Individualism and self-reliance were growing problems at Corinth. Some of the members had come to believe that others within the congregation were dispensable and no longer needed. Why they began to think that way is a matter of speculation (although other parts of Paul's letters give us some strong clues), Paul's emphasis is that each member should value every other member of the congregation because God has placed each one exactly where He wants them inside the body.

The Bigger Picture

Paul continues to emphasize how each member of the local church is a vital part to the everyday functioning of the body. Individualism has been a problem since the fall. Cain displayed it with how he regarded his brother (Genesis 4.9). His disdain for any relationship of care for his brother characterizes the way of the world. Priding ourselves on self-sufficiency and beliefs that we can go at things alone is a philosophy of Satan. It is rooted in the desire to make ourselves our own god.

The Text

NLT:

1 Corinthians 12:21–30

[21] The eye can never say to the hand, "I don't need you." The head can't say to the feet, "I don't need you." [22] In fact, some parts of the body that seem weakest and least important are actually the most necessary. [23] And the parts we regard as less honorable are those we clothe with the greatest care. So we carefully protect those parts that should not be seen, [24] while the more honorable parts do not require this special care. So God has put the body together such that extra honor and care are given to those parts that have less dignity. [25] This makes for harmony among the members, so that all the

members care for each other. ²⁶ If one part suffers, all the parts suffer with it, and if one part is honored, all the parts are glad. ²⁷ All of you together are Christ's body, and each of you is a part of it. ²⁸ Here are some of the parts God has appointed for the church: first are apostles, second are prophets, third are teachers, then those who do miracles, those who have the gift of healing, those who can help others, those who have the gift of leadership, those who speak in unknown languages. ²⁹ Are we all apostles? Are we all prophets? Are we all teachers? Do we all have the power to do miracles? ³⁰ Do we all have the gift of healing? Do we all have the ability to speak in unknown languages? Do we all have the ability to interpret unknown languages? Of course not!

CSB:

1 Corinthians 12:21–30

²¹ The eye cannot say to the hand, "I don't need you!" Or again, the head can't say to the feet, "I don't need you!" ²² On the contrary, those parts of the body that are weaker are indispensable. ²³ And those parts of the body that we consider less honorable, we clothe these with greater honor, and our unrespectable parts are treated with greater respect, ²⁴ which our respectable parts do not need. Instead, God has put the body together, giving greater honor to the less honorable, ²⁵ so that there would be no division in the body, but that the members would have the same concern for each other. ²⁶ So if one member suffers, all the members suffer with it; if one member is honored, all the members rejoice with it. ²⁷ Now you are the body of Christ, and individual members of it. ²⁸ And God has appointed these in the church: first apostles, second prophets, third teachers, next miracles, then gifts of healing, helping, leading, various kinds of tongues. ²⁹ Are all apostles? Are all prophets? Are all teachers? Do all do miracles? ³⁰ Do all have gifts of healing? Do all speak in tongues? Do all interpret?

Explore the Text

1. How are we to regard the "weaker" parts of the body?

2. Are there some practical applications you can make to the day-to-day happenings inside the local church from the analogy Paul uses in 12.22–24?

3. Who put the body together? Why is greater honor given to *the less honorable?*

4. What happens when one member suffers? Or, when one member is honored?

5. For what purpose did God distribute His gifts inside the church?

About the Text

In verses 21–30, Paul continues to stress our mutual dependence on each other. He presses his readers to value each other's gifts, which have been graciously given by the Spirit. What was happening at Corinth was no different than what can happen inside a local congregation today. Some people, due to an inflated vision of themselves, feel they can get along without some other members of the church. Paul, swiftly and concisely, debunks this thinking: *on the contrary, those parts of the body that are weaker are indispensable,* 12.22.

I. **12.21-27—Functioning Together Properly**
   A. 12.21—a few members of the church in Corinth had concluded that the other "less desirable" people in the church weren't necessary. They *overestimated their own importance and underestimated that of other believers.*[5] They ignored two basic principles taught in:
   i. Matthew 18.10: how you view another member of the body is how you view Christ.
   ii. Romans 14.1—15.7: instead of disregarding those who we regard as weak, we are to work for their good, building them up.
   B. 12.22—as we look at the human body, some of the more prominent parts, while very important, it is possible to live without them. People can function without an eye or hand and still live. But a person will not live without his heart or liver. While those body parts may not be visible on the outside, they are vital to the functioning of your body.
   i. The same is true inside the church. While those who occupy the public speaking roles are important, some of the most vital operations of the church take place by those who are not visible.
   ii. Their value should never be questioned. They should be nourished, built up, and protected.
   C. 12.23-27—God has put the body together, giving greater honor to the less honorable.
   i. He did this to prevent division.
   ii. All the members should have the same care for each other. Mutual support and encouragement are desired. They preserve unity.
   iii. There is to be no disdain or rivalry, envy or malice, or inferiority or superiority.
   iv. Members of the church are one in Christ and one in each other.
II. **12.28-30—What God Has Given the Church**
   A. Paul returns to an earlier argument made in the chapter, stressing the need for diversity, not uniformity when it comes to the gifts and ministries of the church.
   B. In v. 28, Paul lists out some of the gifts and ministries of the early church. Some of these gifts were miraculous in nature, others were not. Some of the offices mentioned were exclusive to the early church during the time preceding the complete revelation of Scripture. Other offices and positions of leadership still exist in the church today.
   C. 12.29-30—God does not intend for every member to have the same gift … and not all gifts are intended to be out front

and public in nature. Their response was expected to be with gratefulness and to employ them in faithful use.

Reaction

1. Individualism seems to be built in our DNA. It carries over into how we view others in the church. What is wrong with the thinking that says, "They don't need me?" Likewise, what is wrong with the thinking that says, "I don't need them." What does this type of thinking forget?

2. As you think about your local congregation, what are some of the vital ministries that go on behind the scenes … things that don't receive much attention … but are vital to the life of the church?

3. What can you do to strengthen, protect, and encourage those "less visible" ministries?

4. What type of care are we to have for *each* member of the body?

5. How good are you at being connected with other members of your local congregation? What can you do to improve those connections?

6. Verse 27 brings us back to the big picture. We are all part of the body of Christ. How does keeping this in mind promote unity inside the local church?

7. In the listing of gifts in v. 28, what functions still exist in today's church? Provide a short definition of each. Does your gift fit into any of these functions/ministries?

For the Christian Today

We need to see the indispensability of each member of the local church. Can you imagine any of your body parts declaring they were more important than some of the others and didn't need them? Such a notion is preposterous. Likewise, if we fail to see the great value of others, even the "weakest" members of the body, we are falling into the same trap the Corinthians did. Remember, how we regard others reveals how we regard Jesus Christ, Matthew 18.10. Every Christian has been called to bear the weaknesses of his brother or sister and build them up, encouraging them, Romans 15.1–2, 7.

We need to understand the importance and value of our gift and placement inside the local church. No one wants to be *dispensable*. We do not want to be tossed aside or seen as unimportant. Many people church shop and hop around from congregation to congregation looking for where they will be the right fit. *Where will I be accepted?* Remember, if you are a member of a local church, you are indispensable. And all the other members are indispensable parts of your life. They, like you, are part of the body that God has put together to display the beauty of the gospel.

Mutual care promotes unity. If we are all interdependent upon each other, then we will experience joy and pain as one. If one member suffers, all suffer together. If one member is honored, all rejoice together. Paul also spoke of this mutual care in Romans 12.15–16. Mutual care is the expectation. This is opposed to self-care, which often reflects today's culture. This can be reflected in how we can seek to advance ourselves rather than advancing the interests of others.

How to maintain interdependence is achieved by continually looking to Christ. He could have viewed us as dispensable. Rather, he viewed us through the eyes of grace and saw us as indispensable, so much that he gave himself on our behalf. *He became dispensable in our place.* Let's consider the body analogy again. The most indispensable part—the head—was willingly dishonored so that the *least presentable parts—you and I—might receive honor.* The strongest member was made weak and dispensable in order that the weaker members—you and I—might be considered indispensable. His love has transformed our reality, which in turn should fill our hearts with humility. We are each totally dependent upon Christ and the local church in which He has placed us. We do not need to distinguish ourselves or compete for a higher position. Our position in the body has been secured. Our identity has been given to us by Christ and is affirmed by the other parts of the body.[6]

Pray For …

1. A humble and accurate perspective of yourself and others within the body of Christ, valuing and appreciating every member, treating them with honor, care, and mutual support, and building unity and harmony within the church."
2. Guidance in utilizing the gifts God have given you for the benefit of the body of Christ, opening your heart to embrace diversity and variety, and cultivating a spirit of cooperation and collaboration among the members of the congregation.
3. Wisdom and discernment to leaders and members in identifying and utilizing their gifts effectively within the church, building unity, harmony, and gratefulness as each member embraces their unique strengths and contributes to the advancement of the kingdom.

Journal

What are some things you can do to keep the proper view of yourself (Romans 12.3) as you consider your place in the body and those around you? How can you encourage other members of the body this week?

For Further Study

Read through Matthew 18.1–10 and Romans 14.1—15.7. What are the basic principles presented in these two texts and how do they apply to how God has put the body together?

Lesson 5

If I Don't Have Love

1 Corinthians 13.1–3

Overview

"You people are only about love, love, love …" we often hear in a derogatory manner. And to that I would simply answer, "Yes, we are." Why the emphasis on love? Because God is love, 1 John 4.7–9. And, upon our conversion, the Holy Spirit poured God's love into our heart, Romans 5.5. It is the first of the nine characteristics of the fruit of the Spirit, Galatians 5.22–23. It is the foremost Christian virtue. Without it, as we will see in this lesson, Paul says, our acts of service and ministries are worthless. If Satan can keep us from loving others, then he has succeeded in his mission. It's "Game Over." We don't need to focus less on love, we need to focus more on it.

Through our lifetime we may have known brothers and sisters who have excelled with various talents and gifts but render their actions useless because of a lack of gentleness and love. We may know people gifted in knowledge and wisdom of the Scriptures, but know little about humility, care, and patience with others who may not share their abilities. We may also know someone who gives to others only out of abundance but otherwise, generally cares little about the needy. Though they share in the greatest quantity, without love, it profits one nothing.

The Bigger Picture

In 1 Corinthians 12, Paul begins a three-chapter instruction on the proper usage of spiritual gifts. In Chapter 12 he reminds the Corinthians of the variety of gifts given by the Spirit, the origin of those gifts, and how God has arranged the gifts/members in the body just as He sees fit. In Chapter 14, Paul will describe the proper function of these gifts inside the local church body. Sandwiched in the middle he will speak about the most important element: the atmosphere required for the proper working of the gifts. If we do not move with a spirit of sacrificial and caring love for one another, the gifts and talents we possess will actually become a hindrance to the work of the Lord. This must be avoided at all costs.

The Text
NLT:

1 Corinthians 13:1–3

¹ If I could speak all the languages of earth and of angels, but didn't love others, I would only be a noisy gong or a clanging cymbal. ² If I had the gift of prophecy, and if I understood all of God's secret plans and possessed all knowledge, and if I had such faith that I could move mountains, but didn't love others, I would be nothing. ³ If I gave everything I have to the poor and even sacrificed my body, I could boast about it; but if I didn't love others, I would have gained nothing.

CSB:

1 Corinthians 13:1–3

¹ If I speak human or angelic tongues but do not have love, I am a noisy gong or a clanging cymbal. ² If I have the gift of prophecy and understand all mysteries and all knowledge, and if I have all faith so that I can move mountains but do not have love, I am nothing. ³ And if I give away all my possessions, and if I give over my body in order to boast but do not have love, I gain nothing.

Explore the Text

1. Why do you think Paul first mentions the miraculous gift of tongue speaking in his list of examples of gifts?

2. What is the effect of tongue speaking if one's heart is not motivated by love?

3. What if we have been blessed with a superlative of gifts, talents, and abilities and have no love? Do our works matter? Explain.

4. Why do you think love is so essential to our spiritual life?

About the Text

It has been said that 1 Corinthians 13 serves as a breath of fresh air in the midst of a book that has been so pointed in its correction of disunity, selfishness, sin, and boasting. You have probably heard this chapter quoted in its entirety in many weddings. And while it certainly fits inside the imagery of a marriage, it's placement here, amid a discussion on the abuse of spiritual gifts resulting from selfishness, boasting, and self-seeking ways makes it very powerful. So, if we viewed chapter 12 as Paul's description of the placement and variety of gifts and chapter 14 as describing how to use the gifts correctly, then chapter 13 describes the intended atmosphere in which those gifts operate out of love. It is the *even better way* Paul brought up at the end of chapter 12 (12.31). Conflict, pride, envy, or jealousy have no place in the body … only love.

I. **13.1–3: Love is the Atmosphere in which Spiritual Gifts Operate**
    A. The quality of one's spiritual life is not reflected in the spiritual gifts he or she has received but rather, in the fruit one produces, the first of which is love, Galatians 5.22.
  i. The possession of a spiritual gift does not make one spiritual. Walking in the Spirit is what makes one spiritual. Walking by the Spirit (Galatians 5.16, 25; Ephesians 4.1; Colossians 3.16) describes the lifestyle or day-to-day obedience of the Christian.
  ii. Without the fruit of the Spirit, spiritual gifts have a way of becoming counterproductive.
  iii. The Corinthians had given themselves over to selfish ways where they concentrated first on themselves having little or no regard for others.
    B. 13.1—This is the *agape* love of action and sacrifice. It is wrapped in humility with a commitment to meet the needs

of others. It is void of pride and selfishness, self-glory and vanity.
i. Love is the only proper motivation for ministry and service.
ii. We serve others out of the sacrifice of ourselves to the expectation of God and the sacrifice of our life to meet the needs of others. Any other motivation renders our service useless.
iii. The entirety of 1 Corinthians 13 serves as one of the best definitions in the New Testament on what *agape love* is.
iv. It is a love more concerned with giving than receiving. It is an act of choice that will love even those who are an enemy.
v. 1 Corinthians 16.14: everything a Christian does should be done in love. There is no substitute.
   1. Correct theology and good works are never a substitute for it.
   2. It should be the natural outpouring of who we are because it has been poured into us, Romans 5.5.
C. 13.1—*What We Say:* Gifts of fluent and powerful speaking without love are nothing.
i. If Paul were able to speak with the skill of the greatest public speaker or teacher, it would mean nothing if he did not speak in love.
ii. Paul used this here because it appears that the Corinthians were trying to use their supernatural speaking gifts for their own power and gain. All their speaking had become nothing more than noise.
D. 13.2—*What We Know:* Prophecy, knowledge, and faith without love are nothing.
i. A *motive* is the driving force behind what we say and do. It is the *reason*.
ii. If our *reason* for doing something is motivated by the desire for praise, self-promotion, or creating a personal advantage of some sort, the effectiveness of our ministry will be damaged. We must be motivated by love.
E. 13.3—*What We Do:* Benevolence and even martyrdom mean nothing without love.
i. The focus of acceptable service toward others and even the giving of one's life comes from love. It is always for a spiritual purpose.
ii. It is never about the praise or blessings that may come for doing them.
iii. The loveless person produces nothing, is nothing, and gains nothing.[7]

Reaction

1. What makes a person spiritual? Why should our emphasis focus more on the *fruit of the Spirit* than the *gifts of the Spirit*?

2. What is *agape* love? How does it differ from the other aspects of love as used in the Greek language? (*phileo* or *eros*)

3. Read Romans 5.5. Why should love be a natural outpouring of each Christian?

4. What do we think the Corinthians were doing with their supernatural speaking gifts? How did this render their actions useless?

5. What do we mean by the word *motive*? What is the only proper motive for spiritual service?

6. Performing benevolence or making self-sacrifices must never be about oneself. Describe some improper motives that can render these actions void. What must the desire be *for*?

For the Christian Today

Love is *the* essential element in effective spiritual living. James Olthius once said, "Loving is not merely one thing among others that we are called to do. Love is not an additive. Loving is of the essence of being human, the connective tissue of reality, the oxygen of life."[8] If we take love away, we cannot function in God's kingdom.

1 Corinthians 13.1–3 describes the world without love. In the verses under focus, Paul wants his readers to think of what they say, what they know, and what they do. Eloquent words that are not infused and built on the foundation of love is only noise. Incredible intelligence and knowledge that is void of kindness, humility, and gentleness is unimpressive … and a deterrence to Christianity. Acts of kindness and service that are driven by selfish motives have a way of turning people off. (A great example of this might be around the holidays when people are only inclined to give because of a tax deduction. The rest of the year they wouldn't think about parting with their resources and things.)

Love fills our spiritual life with meaning. It is the supreme Christian virtue. It is the love by which the Father sent Jesus into the world. John 13.1 captures the degree of Jesus' love: *having loved his own who were in the world, he loved them to the end.* The last phrase in the verse is significant. We might could say it another way: "Jesus loved them to perfection," or to the fullest degree or limit. It is the love by which we are to be known:

> I give you a new command: Love one another. Just as I have loved you, you are also to love one another. By this everyone will know that you are my disciples, if you love one another. (John 13:34–35 CSB)

Pray For …

1. A deeper understanding of agape love as the foundation for spiritual gifts and ministry, cultivating this selfless love within your heart to serve others with humility, kindness, and genuine concern, aligning your motives with love rather than self-glory or personal gain.

2. God to expose any areas where you may be seeking praise or personal advantage in relation to your spiritual gifts and knowledge, granting you discernment and self-reflection to ensure that love is the driving force behind your words and deeds, building a genuine desire to serve others with selfless compassion and bring spiritual benefit to those around you.

3. Transformation in your heart so that acts of benevolence or sacrifice are not driven by a desire for recognition or personal gain, but by a deep love for God and others, aligning your motives and actions with His love, that your service may be impactful and bring glory to Him, enabling you to love others unconditionally, imitating the selfless love demonstrated by Christ.

Journal

What are some of the improper motives that we may be tempted to use as we approach our spiritual life? What can we do to fight back and reorient our focus to the only proper motive ... love?

For Further Study

Read John 13.34–35; 15.9; and Romans 13.8–9. What is the supreme mark of our discipleship? What is behind all disobedience to the Lord? What is behind all true obedience? See 1 Corinthians 16.14.

Lesson 6

Love Is …

1 Corinthians 13.4–7

Overview

As Paul opened 1 Corinthians 13, he described the world without love. Without love, the things we say, the knowledge we possess, and the ways we serve are useless. Our words are little more than noise. Our knowledge is nothing. Our acts of service and sacrifice are worthless. Love is *the* essential in the Christian life. Now in verses 4–7, Paul presents the best description of true love that has ever been given. Underlying it all is a growing absence of selfishness. This is the love of choice, that may be exercised in the void of sentimentality or warmth, but nonetheless, it is still practiced. This is the type of love that never gives up. It endures. It loves and loves and loves. It is the type of love with which God loves us. It is the kind of love God expects us to practice inside the church.

Love was a diminishing quality inside the church at Corinth. It was plagued with bitterness, rivalry, arrogance, condescension, and strife. The Christians needed to understand that their incredible blessings and gifts from God could become a source of division and strife if misused in an atmosphere void of love.

The Bigger Picture

Love is produced within us through our surrender to the Spirit. As we work to empty ourselves of our self, the Spirit through His ongoing work of transformation adds love to our life. It is an absolute necessity that we surrender to the Spirit's work. We must not diminish or downplay any teaching on love. It is an essential. It is a basic matter of Christian doctrine. Nothing substitutes for love.

The Text

NLT

1 Corinthians 13:4–7

⁴ Love is patient and kind. Love is not jealous or boastful or proud ⁵ or rude. It does not demand its own way. It is not irritable, and it keeps no record of being wronged. ⁶ It does not rejoice about injustice but rejoices whenever the truth wins out. ⁷ Love never gives up, never loses faith, is always hopeful, and endures through every circumstance.

CSB

1 Corinthians 13:4–7

⁴ Love is patient, love is kind. Love does not envy, is not boastful, is not arrogant, ⁵ is not rude, is not self-seeking, is not irritable, and does not keep a record of wrongs. ⁶ Love finds no joy in unrighteousness but rejoices in the truth. ⁷ It bears all things, believes all things, hopes all things, endures all things.

Explore the Text

1. What is patience? How would you define it as it works inside the context of brotherhood relationships?

2. How is kindness connected to patience?

3. Can love thrive inside an atmosphere of jealousy? Explain. What can prompt our envy and jealousy?

4. What does it mean to "brag?" How can this damage relationships?

5. How do arrogance and rudeness go together? How can we avoid these things?

6. Why do you think love will have difficulty flourishing in a self-seeking environment?

7. Why must we avoid being "irritable?" What can we do to eliminate defensiveness in our relationships?

8. How does keeping a record of wrongs lead to unhappiness and strained relationships?

9. Why should we never take satisfaction from someone else's sin?

10. As you read 13.7, what enters your mind as you think of the type of spirit that underlies our relationships with brethren, our spouse, or other people in general? What are some things you can do to reorient your perspective around the things listed in this verse?

About the Text

These verses are one of the most beautiful illustrations of love ever given. This is love personified. Here in defining love, Paul does so by describing what *love does*. We may not see it in English, but there are 16 verbs used in verses 4–7. Of course, the immediate context revolves around the Corinthian problem of division and strife inside the local church. Love isn't merely a profession; it is bound up in decisive action and attitudes. John said it this way:

> Little children, let us not love in word or speech, but in action and in truth, 1 John 3.18

It has been said that on our best days we wish to give this love and on our worst days we long to receive this love.[9] Certainly we are captivated by the beauty of the love described in this passage. But, it feels as if it is just beyond our reach. So many relationships are characterized by a lack of love. We see strife, envy, people keeping records of wrongs suffered, rudeness, and actually rooting for the failure of others. Despite these things, we keep reaching forward. We keep striving for it by allowing it to impact how we communicate, think, and react. The descriptions of love in 13.4–7 draw us outside of ourselves and fill up our life with joy only God can provide. Love generates hope in hopelessness. It brings life back to lifeless situations.

I. **13.4–7: The Marks of Love**
   A. 1 Corinthians 13.4:
     i. Patience with reference to people. "Long-tempered," "slow to anger," "to suffer long." In relationships, patient love wins out.
     ii. Kindness is the natural result of patience. Kindness is the practice of good will. It is gracious, serving, and generous. It is the opposite of being selfish, jealous, spiteful, and proud.
     iii. Love is void of jealousy, boasting, and arrogance.
       1. Jealousy is an unhealthy desire for what someone else has. It also devolves further when it desires evil for them. This can become very destructive. Jealously puts others down.
       2. To be *boastful* means to talk conceitedly to brag. Bragging builds up oneself. As much as we may detest bragging in others, we are so inclined to brag ourselves.[10] Love is never proud.
       3. *Arrogance* means that you think you have arrived; "big-headed"
   B. 1 Corinthians 13.5:
     i. Love is not rude. This is "unbecoming behavior." Using "poor manners." The feelings and sensibilities of others are not taken

into consideration. It is to be overbearing and crude. It is shameful behavior where one moves in defiance of social or moral standards.

ii. Love is not self-seeking. It is the opposite of selfishness.

iii. Love is not easily angered and does not keep a tally sheet of wrongs suffered.

iv. *Irritable* describes a person who is easy to be aroused to anger, often demonstrated by a sudden outburst of emotion or action. Love seeks not to be provoked. It resists becoming irritated, upset, or angered by things said or done by someone else.

v. *Keeping a record of wrongs* leads to miserableness. Holding on to things is the opposite of forgiveness.

C. 1 Corinthians 13.6:

i. Love does not rejoice in unrighteousness … but rejoices in the truth.

ii. It does not rejoice over evil. It does not gossip about the failings of others. It is not happy when someone else fails. Love looks for mercy and justice … even those who may be counted as enemies.

D. 1 Corinthians 13.7:

i. Love bears, believes, hopes, and endures all things. It holds fast to those it loves.

ii. Love is tenacious in the present and propelled by confidence in the future. This enables a person to live through every circumstance and pour oneself out on behalf of others.

Reaction

1. Why do selfishness and patience not mix? What are some examples where you have had to develop the trait of being "long-tempered" with your brothers and sisters? How did your loving patience pay off?

2. What is so dangerous about jealousy? How can we fight back against its encroachment in the church?

3. Is arrogance and self-promotion a problem in society? Explain. What are you doing to make sure you are not being overly influenced by the world in this area?

4. How can we become less "irritable?" Why is this so detrimental to the practice of love?

5. Why is gossip such a serious sin? How do we often justify our participation in it? How can we more effectively combat gossip in the church?

6. How has your love for another brother or sister gotten you through what otherwise would have been an unbearable situation?

7. Why is cynicism so deadly to the life of a church? How can love defeat it?

For Today's Christian

We must love one another earnestly. One of the primary teachings of 1 Corinthians 13.4–7 is that love keeps going on and on. It never gives up … even in the most difficult of circumstances. Peter speaks of this kind of love in 1 Peter 4.8. He says, *above all, maintain constant love for one another.* This is of supreme importance. When he says to "maintain constant love," he is speaking with intensity. In fact, he used a verb that means to "stretch out; extended; as a rope at full tension." This is a sacrificial love. It is practiced despite there may be an absence of sentimental warmth. It is love despite insult, injury, and misunderstanding. *Love covers a multitude of sins.* It should come to characterize all our interpersonal relationships. All the characteristics mentioned in 1 Corinthians 13.7 should be viewed in conjunction with Peter's writing in 1 Peter 4.8.

Kindness is a much-needed virtue in our family, church, and community. While our world pays lip service to kindness through public service announcements and billboard campaigns, society glorifies vengeance, pay back, rudeness, and retribution. We see it in the movies. It is glorified by the politicians. It is being indoctrinated in our young people in our public schools and state universities. It is seen in the church through religious legalism which leads to arrogance and the trampling of others. All of this stands in contrast to Jesus who came to give rest, Matthew 11.28–30. Everything in the ministry of Jesus shows His deep concern for people. He constantly moved with kindness. No person who needed help was cut off. God could have had Jesus reveal His supernatural ability in all sorts of ways. Why did He choose healing? Not only did it reveal His power, but it also demonstrated *compassion* and *kindness*. It was a direct reflection of His love. May we come to practice this more effectively in our marriage, family, and church!

Everyone longs for love. Once you've experienced the beauty of what love is, you want it more and more. Especially if you've dealt with the real pain that comes in the absence of real love. I once read that the best players in baseball typically are only successful in hitting the ball three out of every ten times. Ted Williams, the legendary hitter for the Boston Red Sox, only hit the ball 34% of the time. Yet he was obsessed with the game of baseball and lost sleep over the pitcher he would face in the next game. The joy he experienced of playing the game—hitting the ball 34% of the time—kept him coming back. We may not always get things right in our relationships … most of the time we strike out. But the experience and joy keep us reaching for it. Therefore, love should shape what we say, how we think, and what we do. Who will you encounter tomorrow? How can we show others the love they need? And what comes from it all? The way to be loved is to love. We will never know compassion or gentleness or patience if we do not love. We will never experience forgiveness until we learn to bear with others and forgive. As Paul says in Colossians 3.14: *above all, put on love, which is the perfect bond of unity.*

Pray For …

1. Grace to cultivate the marks of love described in 1 Corinthians 13:4–7, extending patience, kindness, humility, respect, forgiveness, and a love that rejoices in truth, bears, believes, hopes, and endures all things.

2. God to examine your attitudes and actions considering the marks of love in 1 Corinthians 13:4–7, to convict and transform you where you fall short, enabling you to overcome impatience, unkindness, jealousy, arrogance, rudeness, and selfishness, and cultivate a love that bears, believes, hopes, and endures all things.

3. To be filled with God's love, allowing Him to transform your heart to love as He loves, extending patience, kindness, forgiveness, and genuine care to others. Pray for healing in broken relationships, and for Him to grant you opportunities to demonstrate His love in practical ways, bringing hope and life to those in need.

Journal

To you what is most challenging about Paul's description of love in 1 Corinthians 13.4–7? What are some things you can do to begin more effectively practicing the positives mentioned in the passage? How can you better avoid the negatives Paul brings up?

For Further Study

Read Romans 13.8–10. How is love the fulfilment of the law?

Lesson 7

Love Never Ends
1 Corinthians 13.8–13

Overview

In this text, Paul arrives at the climax of his argument on the superiority of love. Everything else will pass away … but love will remain. In this, the Corinthians who were so focused on obtaining the flashiest of supernatural spiritual gifts, needed to understand they were not seeking the greatest thing. What they were seeking after was temporary. What was permanent concerned them little.

The Bigger Picture

Love was missing from the Corinthian Church. Ungodliness, materialism, pride, selfishness, indulgence, hatred, sexual immorality, jealously, and a whole host of other sins had filled their hearts. It is seen in their division, carnality, litigious behavior, and attitudes towards spiritual gifts. They had been called to point the way to Christ … and instead they were allowing the world to impact their lives. The core spiritual ingredient, love, was missing. When that spiritual virtue is absent, nothing will go right. Someone has said that the presence of love "covers a multitude of sins, 1 Peter 4.8, and that the lack of love causes a multitude of sins." That certainly seems to be the case at Corinth. What they needed (and what we need too) is the greatest of spiritual virtues … love. The quality that most characterizes God Himself should characterize His children.

The Text
NLT

1 Corinthians 13:8–13

[8] Prophecy and speaking in unknown languages and special knowledge will become useless. But love will last forever! [9] Now our knowledge is partial and incomplete, and even the gift of prophecy reveals only part of the whole picture! [10] But when the time of perfection comes, these partial things will become useless. [11] When I was a child, I spoke and thought and reasoned as a child. But when I grew up, I put away childish things. [12] Now we see

things imperfectly, like puzzling reflections in a mirror, but then we will see everything with perfect clarity. All that I know now is partial and incomplete, but then I will know everything completely, just as God now knows me completely. [13] Three things will last forever—faith, hope, and love—and the greatest of these is love.

CSB:

1 Corinthians 13:8–13

[8] Love never ends. But as for prophecies, they will come to an end; as for tongues, they will cease; as for knowledge, it will come to an end. [9] For we know in part, and we prophesy in part, [10] but when the perfect comes, the partial will come to an end. [11] When I was a child, I spoke like a child, I thought like a child, I reasoned like a child. When I became a man, I put aside childish things. [12] For now we see only a reflection as in a mirror, but then face to face. Now I know in part, but then I will know fully, as I am fully known. [13] Now these three remain: faith, hope, and love—but the greatest of these is love.

Explore the Text

1. What things were going to cease and come to an end? How is this contrasted to love?

2. What is the "perfect" that Paul referenced?

3. What is Paul's point as he makes the application, *when I became a man, I put aside childish things…* ?

4. Of faith, hope, and love, which is the greatest? Why?

About the Text

The Corinthians had their eyes on many things but were missing the most important thing. The spiritual gifts they all sought were only temporary. What they truly needed to be seeking was love. It is God's greatest gift.

I. **13.8: Supernatural Spiritual Gifts Will Pass Away**
    A. 1 Corinthians 13.8: *Love never ends.*
      i. Like God, love is permanent. Everything else will pass away, but it will remain. One day our faith and hope will be realized through our eternal reward … yet love will continue to abound and thrive.
    B. Gifts of prophecy, knowledge, and tongues will all go away.
      i. Tongues would *cease.* When the time for their purpose had run out, they would stop.
      ii. Prophecy and knowledge would *come to an end.* God would bring them to an end.

II. **13.9–10: Supernatural Spiritual Gifts Were Only Partial**
    A. Gifts of knowledge and prophecy were only partial regarding understanding God's will, mind, and knowing the understanding of His presence.
    B. The *perfection* of 13.10 could be pointing to the cessation of the supernatural spiritual gifts after the completion of the New Testament, Ephesians 4.11–13; Hebrews 2.1–4.

III. **13.11–12: Supernatural Spiritual Gifts Were Elementary**
    A. With the coming of the Word, Christians would be led into spiritual maturity having complete access to God's revealed will.

IV. **13.13: Love is Eternal**
    A. Here Paul mentions the three greatest spiritual virtues: faith, hope, and love.
    B. One day, faith and hope will be realized … in heaven. But love will remain.
    C. It is the greatest because it is like God. *God is love,* 1 John 4.8.

Reaction

1. What is Paul trying to stress in these verses regarding the superiority of love? What is permanent? What will pass away?

2. In what way were the supernatural spiritual gifts *imperfect*?

3. How were they *elementary?*

4. When will our faith and hope be realized? What will remain?

5. Why is love the greatest spiritual virtue?

For Today's Christian

Love must always be our primary aim. Too often we have our sights set lower on things that will not matter in the long run. We get caught up in present issues, disagreements, and squabbles ... which will matter little years from now. My favorite social media feed has a feature where it will look back on my posts on this day from all the years past. Now, after years have passed, I look at some of those old postings and can't remember the context or meaning behind the problem I felt I needed to address. The problem that appeared so pressing then, matters little now. We must always aim higher ... seeing *the person* more than *the problem.* Only then will we move to address our issues in the spirit of love. Problems can fade away. Love remains.

Pray For ...

1. God to shift your priorities and desires to prioritize love above all else, developing a love that endures and remains steadfast, and for Him to grant you a deeper understanding and experience of His love in your life, guiding you in expressing that love to others.

2. Humility in acknowledging the limitations of human knowledge and for a greater reliance on the Word of God to develop a deeper understanding of God's ways.

3. A growing faith that cultivates a love that reflects unconditional, sacrificial, and enduring love. Ask God to help you grow in your capacity to love others and to align your heart with His.

Journal

In your relationships with brethren, what are some things that challenge you keeping your focus on love? Why do we allow temporary problems and issues to cloud our judgment? What are some things we can do to keep love in view?

For Further Study

The view that *the perfect* in 1 Corinthians 13.10 is referring to the completion of the revealed word is just one of several interpretations of this text. Others hold that *the perfect* has to do with the consummation of the age and time after the End. What are some of the implications of this position? Does it seem to fit more aptly than what has been our traditional interpretation? Explain.

Lesson 8

Welcome Each Other

Romans 14.1–12

Overview

At any moment there are people inside your congregation at all different levels of life: young and old and everything in between. Members of your congregation are also at varying levels of spiritual maturity. Some may have been Christians for over 50 years … others just a few weeks or months. Some may have come out of Catholic backgrounds, others out of denominations, and even others come out of no religious background or training earlier in life. Inside the local church you will find almost every type of personality and preference. We all share differences in what we prefer in dress, the food we eat, how we prefer to be entertained, etc. Some Christians like to hold on to a more traditional approach, while others want absolutely nothing to do with that. All these differences and varying maturity levels can very easily lead to … conflict.

The Bigger Picture

In Romans 14–15 Paul is working to solve the conflict that arises between believers. What he deals with here remains applicable as congregations today are really no different from the early church. One of the most prevalent teachings of the apostles centered around the need to get along well with each other. We might describe these two chapters as "unity in action." Here Paul presents four principles for working together with one another:

1. Romans 14.1–12—be understanding of each other.
2. Romans 14.13–23—build up one another.
3. Romans 15.1–7—please one another.
4. Romans 15.8–13—rejoice with one another.

In this lesson, we'll look at the first principle.

The Text

NLT

Romans 14.1–12

[1] Accept other believers who are weak in faith, and don't argue with them about what they think is right or wrong. [2] For instance, one person believes it's all right to eat anything. But another believer with a sensitive conscience will eat only vegetables. [3] Those who feel free to eat anything must not look down on those who don't. And those who don't eat certain foods must not condemn those who do, for God has accepted them. [4] Who are you to condemn someone else's servants? Their own master will judge whether they stand or fall. And with the Lord's help, they will stand and receive his approval. [5] In the same way, some think one day is more holy than another day, while others think every day is alike. You should each be fully convinced that whichever day you choose is acceptable. [6] Those who worship the Lord on a special day do it to honor him. Those who eat any kind of food do so to honor the Lord, since they give thanks to God before eating. And those who refuse to eat certain foods also want to please the Lord and give thanks to God. [7] For we don't live for ourselves or die for ourselves. [8] If we live, it's to honor the Lord. And if we die, it's to honor the Lord. So whether we live or die, we belong to the Lord. [9] Christ died and rose again for this very purpose—to be Lord both of the living and of the dead. [10] So why do you condemn another believer? Why do you look down on another believer? Remember, we will all stand before the judgment seat of God. [11] For the Scriptures say, " 'As surely as I live,' says the LORD, 'every knee will bend to me, and every tongue will declare allegiance praise to God.' " [12] Yes, each of us will give a personal account to God.

CSB

Romans 14:1–12

[1] Welcome anyone who is weak in faith, but don't argue about disputed matters. [2] One person believes he may eat anything, while one who is weak eats only vegetables. [3] One who eats must not look down on one who does not eat, and one who does not eat must not judge one who does, because God has accepted him. [4] Who are you to judge another's household servant? Before his own Lord he stands or falls. And he will stand, because the Lord is able to make him stand. [5] One person judges one day to be more important than another day. Someone else judges every day to be the same. Let each one be fully convinced in his own mind. [6] Whoever observes the day, observes it for the honor of the Lord. Whoever eats, eats for the Lord, since

he gives thanks to God; and whoever does not eat, it is for the Lord that he does not eat it, and he gives thanks to God. ⁷ For none of us lives for himself, and no one dies for himself. ⁸ If we live, we live for the Lord; and if we die, we die for the Lord. Therefore, whether we live or die, we belong to the Lord. ⁹ Christ died and returned to life for this: that he might be Lord over both the dead and the living. ¹⁰ But you, why do you judge your brother or sister? Or you, why do you despise your brother or sister? For we will all stand before the judgment seat of God. ¹¹ For it is written, **As I live, says the Lord, every knee will bow to me, and every tongue will give praise to God.** ¹² So then, each of us will give an account of himself to God.

Explore the Text

1. Why do you think Paul instructs Christians not to argue about disputed matters?

2. In matters of varying judgment, who does God accept?

3. Who/what is the "weak" brother of Romans 14? Who/what is the "strong" brother of Romans 14?

4. Why should we not judge other believers?

5. To whom will we give an account for our actions?

About the Text

In the Roman church, Jews and Gentiles came together from vastly different religious backgrounds. For the Jew, there were two major parts of the Old Law that touched every part of daily life: dietary restrictions and the observance of special days—which had been prescribed in Leviticus. These laws impacted everything: what a person ate, how food was cooked, how one dressed, the days one celebrated with feasts, and many other things. Simultaneously, Gentiles would have been very familiar with feast days and out of an effort to avoid the appearance of having an association with idols, may have avoided all festivals as well as the eating of meats out of caution that it had been offered in pagan worship. The issues in Romans 14 are not matters of sin or morality—they are issues of preference and judgment.

I. **14.1: Welcome Each Other**
   A. Defining *the weak*.
      i. Because of culture or upbringing, the one who is weak in faith has a certain preference that makes him unable to enjoy the freedom he or she has in Christ. They are narrower and intolerant in their approach to liberty in Christ.
      ii. Conflict arises when the weak Christian looks at the strong believer and accuses them of being too loose and uncareful.
   B. Defining *the strong*.
      i. This is the believer who does not feel constrained by ceremony, tradition, or any non-moral externals ... and understands the liberty he or she has in Christ.
      ii. Conflict arises when this believer begins to despise the weak one as being small minded; untaught; and narrow.
   C. 14.13–19—Tongue speaking stirred up the emotions ... not the mind. Edification cannot happen apart from the mind.
   D. The first imperative in v. 1 is to *welcome* one another. The weak welcome the strong and the strong welcome the weak. This means to "take to yourself, embrace intimately into your own love, communion, and fellowship."
   E. The second imperative is *do not argue about disputed matters*. The weak believer is to be accepted, *but not for the purpose of passing judgment on his opinions*, NASB. The strong do not accept the weak for the purpose of arguing with them. Why?

II. **14.2–4: God receives and sustains both the weak and the strong.**
   A. Some are free to enjoy their liberty, others are unable to enjoy it.
      i. When this is the case, the strong are not to hold the weaker person

in contempt. He or she is not to *look down* on the weak. A brother should never be belittled, disregarded, scorned, or treated with contempt.

    ii. Simultaneously, the weak is not to *judge* the strong. There should never be any condemnation of those who exercise their liberty in Christ.

        B. Why? *God has accepted him,* 14.3c. God receives both the weak and the strong. In matters of judgment, if God has not made it a matter of fellowship, who are we to do so? Both must learn to work together.

        C. 14.4—God sustains them both. The opinion others hold in matters of judgment are not our personal problem. *Who are we to judge another's household slave?* Whatever *we think* doesn't change the other person's standing before God. If a brother belongs to the Lord, he will stand.

III. **14.5–9: Both Weak and Strong Belong to the Lord.**
    A. 14.5—During Paul's time, some were concerned about days. Others weren't. *Let each one be fully convinced in his own mind.*
    B. 14.6—Both have the same motive … bringing *honor* and *thanks* to the Lord.
    C. 14.7—Both the weak and the strong don't do these things for themselves, they do it for the Lord. Both have submitted to His Lordship.
    D. 14.8–9—Both belong to the Lord; both wish to please the Lord. Christ's leadership commands us to not make a rift in the church over matters of judgment. When a Christian chooses to act out of conscience to serve and honor Christ, this should not be condemned.

IV. **14.10–12: The Lord will Judge Every Believer.**
    A. 14.10–11—All will stand before the Lord and give an account. Each one's works will be measured. Secrets will be revealed. We are told not to judge each other, 1 Corinthians 3.12–13; 4.5.
    B. 14.12—A time of accounting will come, our works will be examined, and each will receive the reward God brings.

Reaction

1. What are some matters of judgment we struggle with in the church today?

2. What do the principles in these verses teach us in how to respond?

3. Who does God accept? The weak? The strong? Both? Why?

4. What good is your judgment on *another man's* servant? What point is Paul trying to make here?

5. To whom will we give an account for how we have handled matters of discretion?

For Today's Christian

Remember, the focus here is on matters of preference/judgment and not sin. Matters of sin and doctrine must never be compromised upon. We are to remain true to the revealed truths of God's word. However, many conflicts arise over non-essential things. These things can be stopped if we will practice the principle to *welcome one another*. This means criticism of each other needs to be stopped. It is far better that we love one another.

A closely connected passage for consideration is Galatians 5.13–16: *For you were called to be free, brothers and sisters; only don't use this freedom as an opportunity for the flesh, but serve one another through love. For the whole law is fulfilled in one statement: Love your neighbor as yourself. But if you bite and devour one another, watch out, or you will be consumed by one another. I say, then, walk by the Spirit and you will certainly not carry out the desire of the flesh.* The governing principle *in everything* is to *serve one another in love*. How committed are we to *loving our neighbor as ourselves?*

Today we see people biting and devouring each other over differing approaches to grace and works; differences over how the Lord's Supper is conducted; differences over whether a large congregation is better than a small one; and the list goes on and on. When we fail to apply love, we will, as Paul said, *be consumed by one another.*

So, will we *walk by the Spirit?* Will we look out for the interests of others, considering those issues as more important than our own? How committed are you in making unity happen?

Pray For ...

1. A growing desire for unity and acceptance within the body of Christ, help in embracing others with genuine love and fellowship, help in setting aside personal opinions and the desire to pass judgment, and for God to help you cultivate humility and respect for differing perspectives.

2. God to guard your heart against contempt, judgment, and condemnation towards fellow believers with different perspectives, enabling you to see others through God's eyes, embracing acceptance and mutual support, and building unity within the body of Christ.

3. Help in prioritizing pleasing God over personal preferences, working together with fellow believers, and entrusting matters of judgment to His wisdom and eternal judgment.

Journal

What will you commit to doing this week to receiving a brother or sister you have differences with over matters of judgment? What is an act of love you can demonstrate to them?

For Further Study

Read Ephesians 2.19–22. What does this passage teach us about the bigger picture of the church? Who is the cornerstone? How does this passage teach us about the relevance, importance, and connectedness we have with other members of the local church?

Lesson 9

Build Up One Another

Romans 14.13–23

Overview

How can we handle disagreement within a local congregation when it arises due to conflict between those who understand their freedom in Christ and those who do not feel restricted to exercise their liberty. In Romans 14, Paul has defined the *weak* Christian as one who has not yet reached the sufficient maturity to fully understand the freedom God provides through Christ. This is the person who feels restricted, perhaps because they carry over some of the traditions and habits or things from their former life that bother their conscience. This is the person who may tend to bind where God has not bound, and judge those who do not share their convictions.

When Paul mentions a *strong* Christian, in this context, he is describing the Christian who has reached a point of maturity where they understand the liberty they have in Christ. They are comfortable in enjoying all the good things God has provided. For example, they understand that in and of itself: food is not sinful, working on Sunday is not sinful, having a Christmas tree or exchanging gifts is not sinful, or wearing shorts is not always sinful. Sometimes the strong struggle with those who do not embrace the freedoms they are so comfortable with.

Those who are weak tend to judge the stronger brother. Those who are strong tend to look down on the weaker brother. Sometimes those who are strong feel the need to exercise their liberty—and in doing so offend the weak—which creates conflict, disrupts unity, and undermines the testimony of the local church.

The Bigger Picture

In Romans 14 Paul is dealing with Christians in the local church and the conflict that arises between the weak and the strong. Whenever there is a plurality of humans functioning together, conflict will occur. There are many things that can lead to our disagreement. For example, brethren disagree over how to dress for worship; how to celebrate religious holidays; whether or not to wear a tattoo; what kind of music to listen to; wearing shorts; buying a raffle ticket; or going into a restaurant with a bar.

As always when discussing Romans 14, we must remember that sin is sin. It is wrong to do wrong. Freedom in Christ does not give a person freedom to sin. Sin is not subjective. God clearly defines it in His word. Romans 14 does not give Christians the freedom to tolerate sin.

While we no longer live in a world dominated by a sharp cultural divide as the first century Christians did, the church has always faced the potential for conflict between those weak and strong. Paul's teaching in this chapter is that the strong must be willing to limit their liberty for the sake of the weak. We must not cause our brother or sister to stumble. We must never cause them to be hurt. To do so is to destroy our influence and tear down God's work.

The Text

NLT

Romans 14:13–23

[13] So let's stop condemning each other. Decide instead to live in such a way that you will not cause another believer to stumble and fall.

[14] I know and am convinced on the authority of the Lord Jesus that no food, in and of itself, is wrong to eat. But if someone believes it is wrong, then for that person it is wrong. [15] And if another believer is distressed by what you eat, you are not acting in love if you eat it. Don't let your eating ruin someone for whom Christ died. [16] Then you will not be criticized for doing something you believe is good. [17] For the Kingdom of God is not a matter of what we eat or drink, but of living a life of goodness and peace and joy in the Holy Spirit. [18] If you serve Christ with this attitude, you will please God, and others will approve of you, too. [19] So then, let us aim for harmony in the church and try to build each other up.

[20] Don't tear apart the work of God over what you eat. Remember, all foods are acceptable, but it is wrong to eat something if it makes another person stumble. [21] It is better not to eat meat or drink wine or do anything else if it might cause another believer to stumble. [22] You may believe there's nothing wrong with what you are doing, but keep it between yourself and God. Blessed are those who don't feel guilty for doing something they have decided is right. [23] But if you have doubts about whether or not you should eat something, you are sinning if you go ahead and do it. For you are not following your convictions. If you do anything you believe is not right, you are sinning.

CSB
Romans 14:13–23

¹³ Therefore, let us no longer judge one another. Instead decide never to put a stumbling block or pitfall in the way of your brother or sister. ¹⁴ I know and am persuaded in the Lord Jesus that nothing is unclean in itself. Still, to someone who considers a thing to be unclean, to that one it is unclean. ¹⁵ For if your brother or sister is hurt by what you eat, you are no longer walking according to love. Do not destroy, by what you eat, someone for whom Christ died. ¹⁶ Therefore, do not let your good be slandered, ¹⁷ for the kingdom of God is not eating and drinking, but righteousness, peace, and joy in the Holy Spirit. ¹⁸ Whoever serves Christ in this way is acceptable to God and receives human approval.

¹⁹ So then, let us pursue what promotes peace and what builds up one another. ²⁰ Do not tear down God's work because of food. Everything is clean, but it is wrong to make someone fall by what he eats. ²¹ It is a good thing not to eat meat, or drink wine, or do anything that makes your brother or sister stumble. ²² Whatever you believe about these things, keep between yourself and God. Blessed is the one who does not condemn himself by what he approves. ²³ But whoever doubts stands condemned if he eats, because his eating is not from faith, and everything that is not from faith is sin.

Explore the Text

1. Why should we not judge one another?

2. What is a stumbling block? What are some ways you could cause a brother or sister to stumble?

3. If a person believes something is not right (unclean), what will happen to them if they are forced into doing it?

4. What is the most important thing as we interact with our brethren? (14.15a)

5. What are some of the negatives that can happen when the strong force the weak to violate their conscience? (14.16-19)

6. What is Paul's basic instruction to the weak? (14.23)

About the Text

This new section begins with the word *therefore*, in verse 13. Paul has already established that God accepts both the weak and the strong, 14.3. He already sustains the weak and the strong, 14.4. Both weak and strong belong to God, 14.5-9. And, only the Lord will judge, 14.10-12. Since all these things are true, *therefore let us no longer judge one another*. It is never right to sit in condemnation of each other.

I. **14.13: Don't Cause Your Brother to Stumble**
    A. We should never want to do anything to harm a brother or sister in any way.
    B. How could we cause someone to stumble?
      i. By exercising your liberty in front of a *weaker* brother.
      ii. If you push him or her into something that causes them to violate their conscience, thereby causing them to fall into sin.

II. **14.14-15a—Don't Hurt Your Brother**
    A. *Nothing in itself is unclean.*
      i. Moral evil does not exist in non-moral things.
      ii. In matters of preference, there is no evil in neutral things. But…
    B. *If a person believes something to be unclean, to him it is unclean.*
      i. If they are forced into doing it, *they will be hurt* or *grieved* (ESV).
      ii. The idea is to preserve a clear conscience.

  C. 14.15a—It is not loving to push someone into doing something that causes them to stumble or brings them hurt because they have violated their conscience.
 i. God's desire for us is a fellowship of love and concern for each other.
III. **14.15b—Don't Destroy the One for Whom Christ Died**
  A. "Destroy" is a very powerful word meaning to bring to ruin.
 i. A parallel passage is found in 1 Corinthians 8.8-9.
 ii. We should love our brother or sister enough to be cautious as to how we exercise our liberty in front of them.
  B. Love will not seek to destroy a brother.
  C. Instead of hurting them, we should seek to walk in love.
IV. **14.16-19—Don't Destroy Your Influence**
  A. It is possible to so abuse our freedom in Christ that our good is spoken of as evil by those in the world.
 i. Instead of those in the world seeing a group of people who are admirable or *worthy*, they are looked at with disfavor.
 ii. The world is watching and there are times we must set aside our liberty for their sake.
  B. 1 Peter 2.16: If we want to silence the mouths of our critics, we must be careful not to abuse our freedom.
 i. Romans 14.16—if we damage other people, and the world is watching that happen, how will they ever conclude that they want to be a part of the church?
  C. See also 1 Corinthians 10.27-29.
 i. If we offend the weaker brother, we have discredited the significance of Christian love.
 ii. However, if we offend the unbeliever to show love to the weaker brother, we have demonstrated a significant positive regarding Christianity.
 iii. Love for your brother overrules everything else.
  D. Romans 14.17—this is the point of kingdom living.
 i. We have not been called to show the world how *free we are*, we have been called to show them how *loving we are*.
 ii. The essence of the kingdom is not about eating and drinking, it is about righteousness, peace, and joy in the Spirit.
  1. Righteousness: an obedient, God-honoring life that is conformed to His will. Our concern is not about our rights or liberty, it is about holiness and integrity.
  2. Peace: demonstrating peaceful relationships between people and God and brother and brother. The peace of our

relationships provides powerful testimony to the world.
3. Joy: the personal joy of knowing God, experiencing forgiveness, grace, mercy, and love.
iii. 14.19—*pursue what makes for peace and mutual upbuilding.* All have the responsibility to promote a wonderful fellowship of love.
1. 1 Corinthians 14.12—*seek to excel in building up the church.*

V. **14.20—Don't Tear Down God's Work**
A. If we cause a brother or sister to be offended, we tear down the work of God.
B. The weak believer is also a "work of God."
1. God is at work in every Christian. We must not tear down what God is building up.
2. Our weak brother/sister is someone for who Jesus died, they are part of the kingdom, they have the Spirit, …just like every other Christian.
C. 1 Corinthians 8.13: *therefore, if food causes my brother or sister to fall, I will never again eat meat, so that I won't cause my brother or sister to fall.*
D. We must never tear down what God is building up.

VI. **14.21-23—Don't Flaunt Your Freedom**
A. If you are the strong brother, rejoice in the freedom you have, but keep it between yourself and God. Never flaunt your liberty without caring how you impact others.
B. 14.23—If you are the weak brother, don't go against your conscience, *for whatever does not proceed from faith is sin.*

Reaction

1. According to the passage, why should we avoid causing our brothers and sisters to stumble? What are some examples of how we could cause someone to stumble?

2. What is the significance of understanding that what may be considered clean or unclean can vary based on an individual's beliefs and conscience? How should this understanding shape our interactions with others?

3. Why is it important to avoid destroying those for whom Christ died? How can we demonstrate love and caution in exercising our freedom without causing harm to others?

4. Discuss the potential consequences of abusing our freedom in Christ. How might our actions impact our influence and the perception of Christianity by those in the world?

5. What is the central focus of kingdom living according to Romans 14:17? How does this differ from an emphasis on personal rights and liberty?

6. How can we promote peace and mutual upbuilding within the body of Christ? What practical steps can we take to pursue what makes for peace and to excel in building up the church?

7. Why is it crucial not to tear down the work of God by causing offense or stumbling for our brothers and sisters? How does this perspective impact our attitudes and actions towards others?

8. How should strong believers exercise their freedom without flaunting it or disregarding the impact on others? How can we find a balance between rejoicing in our liberty and caring for the conscience of weaker believers?

9. Reflect on the statement in verse 23: "Whatever does not proceed from faith is sin." What does this mean, and how can we ensure that our actions are rooted in genuine faith?

10. Share personal experiences or insights related to navigating differences in beliefs and practices within the body of Christ. How can we maintain unity and love while respecting individual convictions?

For Today's Christian

Be careful when exercising your liberties in front of weaker brethren. If you push them into something that violates their conscience, it causes them to fall into sin. In the first century, if you were around a Jewish convert who struggled with eating pork because of all the dietary restrictions of the Old Law, and by eating it front of him and encouraging him to eat you cause him anxiety and guilt thinking he has transgressed against God.

Growing up in the south, I remember hearing it was taboo for people to play cards. My grandmother liked to play cards but kept that private. When I moved to the Midwest in 1995, I was amazed at how many Christians played cards. I've never really had a problem with it, but it took some time to get my mind around it. While I may feel that in and of itself one can play cards and not sin, if I knew you came out of a background of struggling with going overboard into wagering and gambling … and now avoid such things at all costs … the last thing I should want to do is encourage you to play, violate your conscience, and thereby sin.

The strong Christian chooses to not practice these things so others will not stumble.

We need to preserve a clean conscience. Let's go back to the application I just used. In the north, it used to be taboo to smoke … but it wasn't that way in the south … in the early 80's I remember Christians going out on the front porch between Bible class and worship to smoke. In the late 90's when I began preaching for a congregation in South Dakota, I had a brother express concern because I moved there from Kentucky where brethren in my congregation grew tobacco … and Christians smoked. He actually tried to make a big deal out of it and make me out to be loose on sin. Now I don't smoke ... and I wouldn't encourage you to smoke. And can we all agree that the sin in smoking is allowing it to control us to the point of addiction and the detriment of our health? Food, in and of itself is not sinful. But the sin that comes from food is gluttony where one begins to live for food and destroys his health. Coffee, in and of itself is not sinful. But if I allow it to control me ... then I have crossed the line.

Paul wrote: *"Everything is permissible for me," but not everything is beneficial. "Everything is permissible for me," but I will not be mastered by anything,* 1 Corinthians 6.12. Now, if I know you have reservations about such things, and I try to lead you into it, saying, "we have freedom," and I lead you to violate your conscience, I have erred. It is not loving to push someone into doing something that causes them to stumble or brings them hurt because they've violated their conscience. God's desire for us is a fellowship of love and concern for each other.

What is the goal? *So, whether you eat or drink, or whatever you do, do everything for the glory of God. Give no offense to Jews or Greeks or the church of God, just as I also try to please everyone in everything, not seeking my own benefit, but the benefit of many, so that they may be saved. Imitate me, as I also imitate Christ,* 1 Corinthians 10.31-11.1. The goal between strong and weak believers is a profound testimony that brings forth ... salvation.

Pray For ...

1. Greater sensitivity and wisdom in exercising your liberty in Christ, prioritizing the well-being and spiritual growth of others over personal freedoms, and to cultivate a heart of love that builds up and supports fellow believers.

2. Help in understanding the value and worth of every individual in the body of Christ, a heart of love that cherishes and protects the spiritual well-being of others, and more opportunities to demonstrate love and respect for your brothers and sisters in Christ.

3. God to instill in you a heart that actively seeks to promote unity and harmony within the body of Christ, prioritizing righteousness, peace, and joy in the Spirit over personal rights and liberties, and for guidance in pursuing what leads to peace and edification.

Journal

Reflect on a situation in your life where you had to navigate differences in beliefs and practices within the body of Christ. How did you handle the situation? Did you prioritize the conscience and well-being of others, or did you lean more towards exercising your personal liberties? How can you strive to imitate Christ's example of selflessness and concern for others in similar situations?

For Further Study

Read 1 Corinthians 10.23–33. What is to be our primary concern when engaging with our brethren? How can we do better in buildup up others?

Lesson 10

Please and Rejoice With One Another

Romans 15

Overview

In Romans 15, Paul speaks to believers who want to push their freedom as far as they can. He also addresses those who have yet to grasp their freedom in Christ. They are fearful of going back into sin. Here, Paul establishes that differences in preference can't be wiped away. Instead, we need to embrace an inward unity that binds us all together through self-denial, the work of edification, and praying for unity.

The Bigger Picture

As we examine Romans 14–15 it is important to remember Paul's overall objective in the section that began in the previous chapter, where he is dealing with certain attitudes and behavior that can cripple the work, influence, and unity of a local congregation. These problems are over personal preferences and the carrying on of traditions, which, when imposed on others, can cause confusion, strife, ill will, and disharmony. Every church has considerable differences in age, education, maturity, personalities, and cultural and religious backgrounds. Some have been raised in the strictest of settings, with the stressing of correct forms and procedures. Others have been raised where there was a spirit of openness and freedom. Some have heard the gospel and been exposed to Biblical teaching for decades. Others may have only heard the gospel recently and only understand the essentials.

The listing of our differences in perspectives and spiritual maturity levels can go on and on. And how we handle ourselves can go on and on. Some have yet to grasp their freedom in Christ. They are afraid of committing some religious offense and surround themselves with self-imposed restrictions. Others have the desire to push their freedom as far as they can. They look at others as being too rigid and restrictive to be useful in the Lord. While the stricter brother feels the liberated brother is undisciplined and headed for error and digression. This is the root of disunity.

The Text

NLT

Romans 15:1–13

We who are strong must be considerate of those who are sensitive about things like this. We must not just please ourselves. ²We should help others do what is right and build them up in the Lord. ³For even Christ didn't live to please himself. As the Scriptures say, "The insults of those who insult you, O God, have fallen on me." ⁴Such things were written in the Scriptures long ago to teach us. And the Scriptures give us hope and encouragement as we wait patiently for God's promises to be fulfilled.

⁵May God, who gives this patience and encouragement, help you live in complete harmony with each other, as is fitting for followers of Christ Jesus. ⁶Then all of you can join together with one voice, giving praise and glory to God, the Father of our Lord Jesus Christ.

⁷Therefore, accept each other just as Christ has accepted you so that God will be given glory. ⁸Remember that Christ came as a servant to the Jews to show that God is true to the promises he made to their ancestors. ⁹He also came so that the Gentiles might give glory to God for his mercies to them. That is what the psalmist meant when he wrote:

"For this, I will praise you among the Gentiles;
I will sing praises to your name."
¹⁰And in another place it is written,
"Rejoice with his people,
you Gentiles."
¹¹And yet again,
"Praise the Lord, all you Gentiles.
Praise him, all you people of the earth."
¹²And in another place Isaiah said,
"The heir to David's throne will come,
and he will rule over the Gentiles.
They will place their hope on him."

¹³I pray that God, the source of hope, will fill you completely with joy and peace because you trust in him. Then you will overflow with confident hope through the power of the Holy Spirit.

CSB

Romans 15:1–13

15 Now we who are strong have an obligation to bear the weaknesses of those without strength, and not to please ourselves. ²Each one of us is to please his neighbor for his good, to build him up. ³For even Christ did not please himself. On the contrary, as it is written, **The insults of those who insult you have fallen on me.** ⁴For whatever was written in the past was written for our instruction, so that we may have hope through endurance and through the encouragement from the Scriptures. ⁵Now may the God who gives endurance and encouragement grant you to live in harmony with one another, according to Christ Jesus, ⁶so that you may glorify the God and Father of our Lord Jesus Christ with one mind and one voice.

⁷Therefore welcome one another, just as Christ also welcomed you, to the glory of God. ⁸For I say that Christ became a servant of the circumcised on behalf of God's truth, to confirm the promises to the fathers, ⁹and so that Gentiles may glorify God for his mercy. As it is written,

**Therefore I will praise you among the Gentiles,
and I will sing praise to your name.**
¹⁰Again it says, **Rejoice, you Gentiles, with his people!** ¹¹And again,
**Praise the Lord, all you Gentiles;
let all the peoples praise him!**
¹²And again, Isaiah says,
**The root of Jesse will appear,
the one who rises to rule the Gentiles;
the Gentiles will hope in him.**

¹³Now may the God of hope fill you with all joy and peace as you believe so that you may overflow with hope by the power of the Holy Spirit.

Explore the Text

1. What is the strong Christian's twofold obligation to the weak?

2. In what way did Christ set the example?

3. What kind of atmosphere does God desire in His church?

4. What is the purpose behind the harmony God desires?

5. What does it mean *to be of one mind and one voice?*

About the Text

There are two groups Paul addresses in this text: Those who are strong and those who *are without strength*. The immediate context identifies who each group was. Those who were strong felt they had the right to eat anything or celebrate certain days above others. Those who were without strength were restricting themselves to vegetarianism out of religious conviction. They also regarded every day as the same. These differences in preference can't simply be dismissed and everyone just move on. *Do not argue about disputed matters,* Paul instructs in 14.1. Why? In the church, some elements of faith and practice will always be under discussion. We will never eliminate all differing points of view and one person's conviction does not necessarily mean it should become corporate practice. Not every matter that comes up for discussion in the church is a matter of salvation. There are simply some matters that cannot be and do not need to be agreed upon. Paul's intention here is not to remove the differences in preference, but to teach Christians how to live with them.

   I.   **15.1a—We are not in this to please ourselves**
        A. This should be the guideline in all non-essentials.
        B. Those who are strong bear the weaknesses of the weak for the purpose of building the other person up in his/her faith.
         i. The aim is for their advancement toward spiritual maturity and the embracing of the freedom they have in Christ.
        ii. It was never intended that those without strength continually remain in that condition. The weak should never be content with

being weak. They should never be proud of the positions they hold.
            iii. The expectation is for their spiritual growth and the embracing of the liberties they have in Christ.
                C. The strong must be patient with these weaknesses with a spirit of joy because it is done with the intention of leading the other to maturity.
II.   **15.1b–5—How to live with differences in preference**
            A. 15.1b, 3–4—**embrace self-denial.** The priority for every Christian is *not to please yourself.*
       i. We live to please others for their good and spiritual development.
      ii. 15.3—*for even Christ did not please himself.*
     iii. He took on the reproach of others so that good would come.
     iv. As we become more like Jesus, we grow in aspects of becoming self-denying servants of love.
      v. 15.3b comes from Psalm 69.9 and serves as the basis for what Paul says in 15.4.
                1. Scripture has the power to transform our heart.
                2. It is what produces our endurance and encouragement.
            B. 15.2—**practice edification.** *Each one of us is to please his neighbor for his good, to build him up.*
       i. What will build the faith of my brother?
      ii. What will help him live more by faith?
     iii. How can I help the person without strength to develop strength?
     iv. If I regard myself as strong, how can I avoid a condescending attitude?
      v. Everyone is to move with edification in mind.
            C. 15.5—**engage in prayer.** *Now may the God who gives endurance and encouragement grant you to live in harmony with one another according to Christ Jesus.*
       i. The prayer is for harmony.
      ii. How often do we pray for congregational unity? Togetherness? A mind to work together?
III.   **15.6.—Authentic Worship**
            A. All of this is for the purpose of bringing glory to the Father.
            B. When we live together with the shared values of building each other up and self-denial, our worship will be genuine.
            C. We do this in *one mind.* Shared values, not shared preferences. The idea is to overcome the non-essential things that divide us and work toward experiencing and expressing unity in the spiritual values we hold dear.

IV. **15.7—Welcome One Another**
   A. 15.7: *Therefore welcome one another, just as Christ also welcomed you, to the glory of God.*
      i. "Welcome," CSB; "Accept," NASB. It means to "pull very close to yourself."
      ii. We don't accept others by begrudgingly putting up with them.
      iii. We welcome them as we welcome others with hospitality, bringing them into a place of warmth and closeness.
         1. We are to receive … even if a person comes from a different culture of lifestyle.
         2. We are to receive … even if a person doesn't feel he has the same liberty as we do.
         3. We are to receive … even if some of his view on matters of judgment may be different from our own.
   B. Just as Christ welcomed you…
      i. Jesus is the pattern and example to follow, Matthew 11.29.
      ii. He is our model, Ephesians 4.32; Luke 15.2.
V. **15.8–12—All Have Equality in Salvation**
   A. 15.8–9—The Gentiles have equality in salvation.
   B. 15.10–12—God has always wanted us to be one. All are loved by God.
   C. 15.13—Paul's desire is for Christians to overflow with hope by the power of the Spirit. He wants us to know forgiveness, peace, hope, love, and how to have a right relationship with others. His prayer is that we be fully satisfied in Christ.

Reaction

1. According to the text, what are the two groups of people that Paul addresses? How would you define each group?

2. Why does Paul instruct the believers not to argue about disputed matters? What is his intention in addressing these differences in preference?

3. In what ways can the strong bear the weaknesses of the weak for their

spiritual advancement? How does this promote unity within the body of Christ?

4. What does it mean to embrace self-denial according to the text? How does Christ serve as an example of self-denial?

5. How can practicing edification contribute to building up the faith of others? What should be our focus when considering the needs of our brothers and sisters in Christ?

6. Why is prayer for congregational unity important? How can prayer help us to live in harmony with one another?

7. What does authentic worship look like according to the text? How does living together with shared values contribute to genuine worship?

8. How does the concept of "welcoming one another" align with Christ's example of acceptance? In what ways can we actively practice this in our interactions with others?

9. How does the equality of salvation among all believers, regardless of their backgrounds or preferences, contribute to the unity of the body of Christ? How does this understanding impact our relationships with one

another?

10. What is Paul's desire for Christians as expressed in verse 15.13? How can we overflow with hope and experience satisfaction in Christ?

For Today's Christian

Not everything we think must be voiced. The priority for every Christian is *not to please yourself,* 15.1. This concept goes completely against everything we have been raised with in American culture. We live in a time right now where every person lives to please himself. Our age is characterized by every person getting to express:

- every opinion
- every complaint
- every position

Everything is posted with reckless abandon through social media. *Because our position is best. We've come to our own conclusions. Our experience is what matters.* How much are we getting caught up in this? The priority is not to please yourself. Our goal is to please others for their good and spiritual development.

We must seek to please others so they can be built up. In 1 Corinthians 14, Paul is dealing with problems in the Corinthian worship service. The principle undergirding everything Paul envisions is edification:

- 1 Corinthians 14.26b—*everything is to be done for building up.*
- 1 Corinthians 14.31b—everything is to be done for the purpose *that everyone may learn and everyone may be encouraged.*
- 1 Corinthians 14.33a—*God is not a God of disorder but of peace.*

Now let's look at a more general passage.

- 1 Thessalonians 5.11—*encourage one another and build each other up...*

These admonitions are for every brother and sister in the church family ... not just for those who are spiritually mature. Everyone moves with these purposes in mind.

We work together with one voice. This is the outer form of unity where, despite our differences in preferences, we learn to work together and focus on the same mission. That is the work of Christ in impacting the world with the gospel of Christ; the work of building up and leading each other to spiritual maturity. The aim is overcome the non-essential things that divide us and work toward experiencing and expressing unity in the spiritual values we hold dear.

We need to welcome others, just like Christ has welcomed us. Christ welcomed us while we were unlovely, while we hated God, while we were stained with sin, Romans 5.6-10. Since Christ has not refused to:

- welcome us
- embrace us
- forgive us
- call us His friend
- call us his brother/sister
- empower us
- live within us
- call on us to assist him in telling others about him …

Shall we not welcome one another? If we fail to open our heart to another believer because we resent them, then that is an affront to Christ. If we place restraints on our love to one another … we are violating the principle here. We are violating the example of redemptive action in the person of Christ himself. Remember, Jesus received you *for the glory of God*, 15.7. And this is the same reason we receive one another.

Pray For …

1. For God to grant you a heart of selflessness and humility that prioritizes the spiritual growth and well-being of your brothers and sisters in Christ, the strength and joy to bear with the weaknesses of others and help in guiding them toward maturity in their faith. Ask God to provide you with opportunities to encourage and support them.

2. Guidance in practicing self-denial and edification, pleasing your neighbors for their good and building them up in the faith, cultivating genuine concern without condescension, and the wisdom and discernment to strengthen the faith of those around you."

3. For a spirit of harmony and togetherness within your local congregation, prompting fervent prayer for the unity of believers, for God's guidance and intervention in resolving conflicts and building stronger relationships, so that your congregation's worship and interactions may

bring glory to God and reflect the love and acceptance demonstrated by Christ.

Journal

Reflecting on the passage, consider the cultural influences and societal norms that prioritize self-expression and individual opinions in today's world. How have you been caught up in this mindset, where personal satisfaction and asserting your own beliefs take precedence? In what ways has social media contributed to this phenomenon?

Examine your own actions and attitudes. Are you striving to please others for their good and spiritual development? How intentional are you in seeking to build others up and promote unity within the church? Are there any barriers or restraints on your love for fellow believers that need to be addressed?

Furthermore, think about the concept of welcoming others as Christ welcomed us. How has Christ's unconditional love and acceptance impacted your life? Are there any individuals within the church family whom you struggle to welcome due to resentment or personal biases? How can you align your heart with the example of redemptive action shown by Christ and open yourself to genuinely receive and embrace others?

For Further Study

Read Romans 15.5 again. Paul is still speaking to the Roman brethren, but he also understands his personal desires for them go beyond human ability. So, Paul prays for the action of God. God will answer our prayer by giving us the strength to endure and the ability to encourage. How often do you pray for unity? Will you commit to doing it more?

Lesson 11

Keeping the Unity of the Spirit

Ephesians 4.1–3

Overview

The Christian life should be characterized by selfless love for others, just as Christ demonstrated while on earth. In these verses Paul commands Christians to live the life. He then explains how to live the life, going into detail about the basic attitudes that govern the way we treat our brothers and sisters. These lead us to practice unity through working toward peace inside the body.

The Bigger Picture

Many Christians equate unity to external practices which leads to the idea of unity via uniformity. This viewpoint will always lead to failure. Instead, unity occurs inside the environment Christ and the Spirit have created and is kept and sustained through the desire for peace.

The Text

NLT

Ephesians 4:1–3

[1] Therefore I, a prisoner for serving the Lord, beg you to lead a life worthy of your calling, for you have been called by God.

[2] Always be humble and gentle. Be patient with each other, making allowance for each other's faults because of your love.

[3] Make every effort to keep yourselves united in the Spirit, binding yourselves together with peace.

CSB

Ephesians 4:1–3

¹Therefore I, the prisoner in the Lord, urge you to walk worthy of the calling you have received,

²with all humility and gentleness, with patience, bearing with one another in love,

³making every effort to keep the unity of the Spirit through the bond of peace.

Explore the Text

1. What does "walking" mean in Paul's writing? Where are some other places in the New Testament where he uses the work "walk" or "walking"?

2. What is the "calling" we have received?

3. How are the four qualities of verse 2 progressive and interconnected? Can you have one without the other?

4. Do we create unity or maintain it? If we don't create it, who gave it to us?

5. How do we keep the unity we have been given?

About the Text

The first three chapters contain Paul's doctrinal instruction as he exhorts Christians to embrace their identity in Christ, rest in the salvation they have received by grace, and trust in the unity with other believers from different cultures and backgrounds made possible by Jesus. Now, the last three chapters demonstrate the appropriate response to his instructions. Paul says that Christians are to *walk worthy of the calling they have received.* In other words, Christians are to match their life to the character of Jesus Christ. He has changed our life. Now we exercise the good behavior that comes from it.

The theme of the last three chapters is "walking." Christians walk in unity, 4.1–16. Christians walk in uniqueness, 4.17–32. Christians walk in love, 5.1. They walk in light, 5.8. Christians walk in wisdom, 5.15. They also walk in the Spirit, 5.18. And they walk in warfare, 6.10–13.

I. **4.1: Walk Worthily**
   A. "Worthy" carries the meaning of counterbalancing. In other words, there should be a growing harmony between who you are and how you live. Your life pattern should match your identity. Honoring Christ is part of daily life.
   B. "Calling" is the transformed way of life and walk with God that comes through salvation in Christ.
      i. It is a *high calling,* Philippians 3.14 ASV.
      ii. It is a *holy calling,* 2 Timothy 1.9.
      iii. It is a *heavenly calling,* Hebrews 3.1.
      iv. Such a calling demands a proper response.

II. **4.2: How to Walk**
   A. Notice how Paul first discusses the cultivation of what is within. Attitude first. *Then* doctrine and practice. Jesus is after who we are … which will lead to correct action and practice.
   B. 4.2: Four basic attitudes:
      i. Humility. Older translations use *lowliness* here. Humility involves seeing yourself for who you really are, in light of Christ, and in comparison, with the Father.
      ii. Gentleness. This is a mild disposition that is not prone to retaliation. It is the opposite of being hard, rough, or violent. In some places the word is used to picture a gentle breeze, as in something that would cool a person down on a warm day. It describes the human spirit that has been tamed and is now under control of Christ.
      iii. Patience. Think "long-suffering." There are many different circumstances where we may have to exercise patience:

            1. In negative circumstances
            2. With people
            3. In accepting God's plan for our life
        iv. Forbearing love. To forbear means to suppress with silence. It conveys the idea of throwing a blanket over sin. (See 1 Peter 4.8 and Proverbs 10.12.)
            1. It is the type of love that has room for failures.
            2. It is the fulfillment of Matthew 6.14–15; Luke 6.28–29.
        C. Each of these are progressive.
    i. Humility leads to gentleness.
    ii. Gentleness leads to patience.
    iii. Patience leads to forbearing love.
III. **4.3: This Results in Unity.**
    A. We are to *make every effort* to keep unity. Full time task. Total effort. It is learning in humility how to love each other.
    B. We *keep* the unity of the Spirit.
    i. We don't make, produce, or build it. The Holy Spirit created it when He made us one, 1 Corinthians 12.13.
    ii. It is personal and spiritual.
        C. Unity is held together by *peace*.
    i. Paul uses the imagery of a belt.
    ii. Peace pulls everything together.

Reaction

1. Describe the calling of verse 1. How is it special? Why should we treat it as such?

2. Why is it important to see as Paul describes how to walk that he does not begin with externals? Will the things we do in the Lord's name be effective if we have an improper attitude? Explain.

3. What can we connect from the beatitudes with walking in humility?

4. How do you know if you are a gentle person?

5. How is Jesus the perfect example in demonstrating patience? In bad circumstances? With people? In accepting God's plan? What can we learn from His example?

6. What type of view toward oneself must occur before we can effectively practice forbearing love?

7. What are some things you can do to promote peace within the local body?

For Today's Christian

If self is at the center, we will never know unity. When we dwell upon our feelings, our prestige, our rights, and our place, unity will never happen. Everything Paul speaks about in these verses involves the doing away of self. There is not any other option.

Unity is a gift, not a product. If we look primarily at externals, form, and practice, we will begin to believe unity is achieved by uniformity … that we are the ones practicing it through compliance. This is not the Biblical model. Remember, when Jesus looks at the church, He sees blood-bought believers that He justified Himself. See Romans 8.30. He looks at us as those who He is presently working in for the purpose of ongoing sanctification. Ultimately, He looks at us as the people He is leading to be glorified for all eternity. May we all come to see each other through the eyes of Jesus, not with our human preferences and preferred ways of doing things.

Unity takes the first step. Someone once said, *unity occurs as naturally as a* *two-year-old who shares.* This is why Paul says we need to make every effort to keep it. We are called to love others first and to celebrate the good God is doing in them, rather than waiting for them to come to us when they have figured out where we stand theologically or philosophically. Christians need to be the ones who make every effort to engage others and build bridges … not putting up walls and burning bridges. God has called on us to do this. Will we have the faith to follow?

Pray For …

1. A deeper understanding of your identity in Christ and the transformative power of salvation, for help to align your life with the character of Jesus, cultivating humility, gentleness, patience, and forbearing love in your daily walk.

2. Guidance in developing a humble and gentle spirit, overcoming tendencies towards retaliation, responding with gentleness and patience towards others, and embracing imperfections with forbearing love, reflecting the character of Christ.

3. Help in developing a deep sense of unity within your local congregation, help in prioritizing unity, building love, harmony, and understanding, and allowing the spirit of peace to guide your interactions and relationships.

Journal

What can you do this week to promote unity within the congregation? Is there someone in the congregation you need to make peace with? What measures can you take beginning this week to build a bridge to restore the relationship?

For Further Study

Another passage to consider in tandem with this lesson is Paul's writing in Colossians 3.11–17. Take a few moments to read through that passage and note the progression: We are to put off the old person and put on the new. We do so by understanding our identity as God's beloved. God's holy person is characterized by loving attitudes. We submit to the rule and authority of Christ and are committed to doing everything in His name.

Lesson 12

What Makes Us One?

Ephesians 4.4–6

Overview

As Paul addresses the Ephesians, he is very aware of the wide range of personalities and temperaments among his readers, who would have come from very diverse social and ethnic backgrounds. Now, as members of the Lord's body, he wants all believers (including us) to focus more on the spiritual foundation that unites them. The presence of the Spirit, Lord, and the Father completely transcend any human differences of background, education, culture, etc.

As we review the verses leading up to our study today, we remember that Paul has called for us to *walk worthy of the calling we have received,* 4.1. In other words, we must live the life. Next, Paul speaks about *how* to walk worthy by discussing the attitudes that must be developed in the inner self, 4.2–3. Verses 7–11 shows us how, to walk worthy, we need to take advantage of the resources God provides by embracing the great diversity of *gifts* God has given as well as the gifted men who equip saints for the work of ministry, 4.7–11. As saints do the work of ministry, the body is built up, spiritual maturity comes about, doctrinal stability results, loving evangelism happens, which all leads to growth, 4.12–16.

The foundation for it all rests in verses 4–6. The seven ones serve as the basis for our spiritual life and unity with God and other believers.

The Bigger Picture

The verses in our text are not to be seen as a formal creed of the church, but they clearly are a collection of statements that would have been readily affirmed by those inside the early church. Paul has similar statements in 1 Corinthians 8.6, where he speaks of one God and one Lord, and, 1 Corinthians 12.4–6, where he speaks of the same Lord, Spirit, and God.

Some believe these verses are a fragment of an early Christian hymn.[11]

The Text

NLT

Ephesians 4:4–6

⁴For there is one body and one Spirit, just as you have been called to one glorious hope for the future.

⁵There is one Lord, one faith, one baptism,

⁶one God and Father of all, who is over all, in all, and living through all.

CSB

Ephesians 4:4–6

⁴There is one body and one Spirit—just as you were called to one hope at your calling—

⁵one Lord, one faith, one baptism,

⁶one God and Father of all, who is above all and through all and in all.

Explore the Text

1. Why do you think Paul uses the word "one" so much in these verses? What is the point?

2. Do you think there is any significance to there being 7 "ones" here? If so, why? If not, why not?

3. What is the body Paul refers to?

4. What is our one hope?

5. What is the *one faith* Paul refers to?

6. Why do you think Paul mentions baptism here?

About the Text

Ephesians 4.4–6 serves as a type of bridge between Paul's call for unity in verses 2–3 and his discussion of diversity that begins in verse 7. Everything here needs to be viewed with unity in mind. Christians are one spiritually with the Spirit, Lord, and Father and are one with one another. Here, Paul speaks of the marks of oneness that are basic to our doctrine and life.

I. **4.4: Unity in the Spirit**
    A. One Body
      i. The "body" is the church, which is made up of individual believers in Christ. When we think of the church, this is where our minds should go first … not to an institution or hierarchy or organization.
      ii. There is only one. The unity of this body is at the core of Paul's writing in Ephesians, see especially 2.11–22. All the things that would typically divide human beings have been taken away (ethnic, race, gender, etc.).
      iii. The unity we enjoy should rise above any human association or society that has its grounding in this world.
    B. One Spirit
      i. The Spirit dwells inside the believer and serves as the unifying force in the body. *In him the whole building, being put together, grows into a holy temple in the Lord. In him you are also being built together for God's dwelling in the Spirit*, Ephesians 2.21–22.
      ii. The Spirit creates, fills, coordinates, orchestrates, and empowers the body of Christ.[12]
      iii. All who are members of the one body are that because of the Spirit of God dwelling in them, Romans 8.9.
    C. One Hope
      i. The *hope of our calling* is our ultimate perfection and glory through Christ. (Ephesians 1.4; Romans 8.29)

    ii. We will realize our hope when we see Him face to face, 1 John 3.2. Christ is the *hope of our glory,* Colossians 1.27.

    iii. The receiving of this hope is guaranteed by the Spirit, Ephesians 1.13–14.

II.   **4.5: Unity in Christ**

    A. One Lord

    i. Jesus is the object of our faith, Ephesians 3.12.

    ii. He is *the way,* John 14.6; salvation is *in no other,* Acts 4.12; He is *Lord of all,* Romans 10.12.

    iii. Where there is the same Lord, all (black/white; rich/poor; great/small) are yoked together.

    B. One Faith

    i. This is the set of teachings handed down in the word of God, which all have their basis in the common belief in Christ.

    ii. References to "the faith" abound in Paul's later writing in the Pastorals,[13] and there is a reference to *the faith* in Jude 3, of which we are to *contend for.*

    C. One Baptism

    i. Baptism is an experience every Christian shares. Christians are baptized *into Christ,* Galatians 3.27. It is certainly a unifying experience.

    ii. Baptism is the moment believers are placed into the body by the Spirit, Titus 3.4–6. It is at baptism where the believer confesses Jesus as Lord.

III.   **4.6: Unity in the Father**

    A. One God and Father of all…

    i. Ultimately, our unity is possible because of the Father, who is the Father of us all. See also 1 Corinthians 8.6; 12.5–6. We are all His creatures, made in His image, and part of His family due to His love, Ephesians 1.5.

    ii. Christians believe that they *live in a God-created, God-controlled, God-sustained, God-filled world, and even more, that God indwells them and is working out His purpose through them.*[14]

    B. God is *above all, and through all, and in all.*

    i. This is referencing the unity that God gives us through the Spirit and His Son. We are one people through our God who oversees everything, omnipotent, and omnipresent.

    ii. We are all family because of the enduring plan of the Father.

Reaction

1. Why is it important to think about *people* when we think of the church? Why is it so easy to let our minds dwell toward an *institution* when thinking of the church?

2. What role does the Spirit play in our oneness?

3. What is the hope of our calling?

4. Who is *the* object of our faith?

5. What is *the faith*?

6. What brings us together in baptism?

7. What does Ephesians 1.5 say about the Father, from who our unity originates?

For Today's Christian

The Spirit brings unity. Through His work, all believers are made alive spiritually on the occasion of their baptism, Titus 3.4–6. Spiritual life is being granted to all types of people from every imaginable background, culture, status, or citizenship. Every possible wall a man or woman could erect, the Holy Spirit has torn down. We are *being built together for God's dwelling in the Spirit,* Ephesians 2.22. We need to see the significance of the Spirit's work, respect it, and live inside of it. Every day, we need to *make every effort* to promote peace, 4.3.

The Lord ministers in unity. He is the object of our faith, 1 Corinthians 8.6. One day every tongue will confess that He is Lord, Philippians 2.11. Our faith is rooted in the Word of the Lord, which has been *delivered once and for all to all the saints,* Jude 3. It is for this faith we are to contend. And it is in Him that we have been baptized, Galatians 3.26–27. Every Christian has the same start … in the waters of baptism. It is an experience that should draw each one of us together.

The Father works in unity. All Christians have the same Father. We are family. Brothers and sisters, each with a common start, a shared destiny, all made possible by the love of the Father, Ephesians 1.5; John 3.16. The beauty of it all is that while we all may be very different … we all share the same identity … and that alone should bring us together in unity and love.

Pray For …

1. A deeper understanding and experience of the unity in the Spirit, Christ, and the Father within the body of Christ, helping you value and prioritize unity, promoting harmony, love, and cooperation among fellow believers.

2. Greater faith in Jesus Christ as the one Lord and the object of your faith and salvation, enabling you to hold firm to the teachings of the faith and live out your spiritual commitment in a way that reflects unity and shared identity with fellow Christians.

3. "Dear God, deepen my sense of connection and relationship with You as my heavenly Father, guiding me to live a life that reflects Your character and purposes, walking in unity with fellow believers and aligning my thoughts, words, and actions with Your divine plan for unity among Your people."

Journal

As you go about this week, write down some of the things that God has done to make you one with other believers. For example, you share the same ....

Since this is the case, why do we have division in the church? What do you think God thinks about this?

For Further Study

Explore the New Testament for other passages that speak of God's love for us in His great desire to save us from sin.

Lesson 13

Standing Firm in One Spirit

Philippians 1.27—2.4

Overview

This section of Paul's writing begins a line of thinking that runs through the end of chapter 3. The well-known verses of 3.20–21 form a fitting conclusion for the point Paul wants to make:

> Our citizenship is in heaven, and we eagerly wait for a Savior from there, the Lord Jesus Christ. He will transform the body of our humble condition into the likeness of his glorious body, by the power that enables him to subject everything to himself.

Here, we learn how citizens of the heavenly realm are to live on earth. We live for the good of others and in partnership with other believers. We strive for consistency with Christian values and live with a sense of pride in our new identity. And we are to constantly interact with fellow believers who are on the same journey to heaven.

The Bigger Picture

Most all the early Christians had trouble and persecution because of their decision to follow Christ. The Philippians were no different. They were experiencing stress and opposition to their Christianity. Those who stand and endure together have a way of blending together. Difficult times are opportunities to grow together in unity, not be driven apart.

The Text

NLT

Philippians 1:27—2:4

[27] Above all, you must live as citizens of heaven, conducting yourselves in a manner worthy of the Good News about Christ. Then, whether I come and see you again or only hear about you, I will know that you are standing together with one spirit and one purpose, fighting together for the faith, which is the Good News.

[28]Don't be intimidated in any way by your enemies. This will be a sign to them that they are going to be destroyed, but that you are going to be saved, even by God himself.

[29]For you have been given not only the privilege of trusting in Christ but also the privilege of suffering for him.

[30]We are in this struggle together. You have seen my struggle in the past, and you know that I am still in the midst of it.

[1]Is there any encouragement from belonging to Christ? Any comfort from his love? Any fellowship together in the Spirit? Are your hearts tender and compassionate?

[2]Then make me truly happy by agreeing wholeheartedly with each other, loving one another, and working together with one mind and purpose.

[3]Don't be selfish; don't try to impress others. Be humble, thinking of others as better than yourselves.

[4]Don't look out only for your own interests, but take an interest in others, too.

CSB

Philippians 1:27—2:4

[27]Just one thing: As citizens of heaven, live your life worthy of the gospel of Christ. Then, whether I come and see you or am absent, I will hear about you that you are standing firm in one spirit, in one accord, contending together for the faith of the gospel,

[28]not being frightened in any way by your opponents. This is a sign of destruction for them, but of your salvation—and this is from God.

[29]For it has been granted to you on Christ's behalf not only to believe in him, but also to suffer for him,

[30]since you are engaged in the same struggle that you saw I had and now hear that I have.

[1]If, then, there is any encouragement in Christ, if any consolation of love, if any fellowship with the Spirit, if any affection and mercy,

[2]make my joy complete by thinking the same way, having the same love, united in spirit, intent on one purpose.

[3]Do nothing out of selfish ambition or conceit, but in humility consider others as more important than yourselves.

⁴Everyone should look not to his own interests, but rather to the interests of others.

Explore the Text

1. What did Paul desire to hear about the Philippian church?

2. What does it say about their identity? Why is understanding who we are so essential to unity?

3. What kind of resistance were the Philippian Christians receiving? How were they to respond?

4. What is Paul trying to remind the Philippians of in 2.1?

5. What does it mean to *think the same way*? Does this mean unity by uniformity?

6. Who does our love focus upon? (2.2)

7. What is our *one purpose*?

8. What is the underlying attitude that makes unity work?

About the Text

During Paul's time the Greco-Roman world held that the highest honor was to be a Roman citizen. Philippi was a Roman colony and was Roman in every way. This included the Roman lifestyle, attitude and mindset, language, names, and everything else. It was believed that as a culture, they had been refined to the highest standard in history up to that point. To be a citizen meant you did not live for yourself. You lived for the good of the emperor and his empire.

In our reading we see how Paul calls believers to live for the good of others, in partnership with other believers, and in consistency to the values of Christ.

I. **Philippians 1.27b–30: Four Things Christians Do Together**
   A. 1.27: *Stand firm in one spirit.*
      i. Spiritual character is in view. Involves godliness, purity, holiness, and obedience.
      ii. Christians work together to encourage each other in these things, Hebrews 3.13.
   B. 1.27: How do we stand together? *In one accord.*
      i. This is directed out by our attitude. Selfishness always brings disunity.
      ii. Our attitude must be one of sharing, humility, and oneness.
   C. 1.27: *Contending together for the faith of the gospel.*
      i. Unity with a purpose. We have a common opponent to face, and our objective is to win. Our common objective is victory over Satan.
      ii. Someone has said, *the army that faces death doesn't have any internal quarrels. It is only concerned about defeating death. Petty internal conflicts are lost in the battle for what really matters.*
      iii. We proclaim and preach *the faith of the gospel.* We preserve it and proclaim it.
         1. We do this not being frightened by our opponents ... we are called to be bold and courageous because victory is ours.
   D. 1.29–30: *Suffer together.*

  i. God has graciously gifted us with suffering.
  ii. Suffering leads us to heaven; strengthens the church; and wins the lost.
II. Philippians 2.1: Four Motives for Unity
 A. 2.1a—Our *encouragement* in Christ.
  i. Each of us receive personal and consistent help from Christ through His forgiveness, strength, wisdom, and blessings.
 B. 2.1b—Our *consolation of love.*
  i. We have received an overflowing amount of love, Romans 5.5.
  ii. It has come at its greatest, highest, and most superior level.
 C. 2.1c—Our *fellowship with the Spirit.*
  i. Galatians 3.3—we are born by the Spirit.
  ii. Galatians 5.16—we walk by the Spirit.
 D. 2.1d—Our *affection and mercy.*
  i. When we fall, the Spirit picks us up. When we sin, the Spirit forgives. When we need strength, he supplies it. When we need wisdom, he gives it.

III. Philippians 2.2: Four Identifiers of Unity
 A. 2.2a—*Thinking the same way.*
  i. Unity comes when believers think alike, i.e., have the same attitude.
  ii. Believers need to come to hold the same feeling, disposition, attitude, and thinking patterns.
 B. 2.2b—*Having the same love.*
  i. Everyone is loved the same. Mutual self-sacrifice.
  ii. See Romans 12.10.
 C. 2.2c—*United in spirit.*
  i. "one-souled." Deep harmony and passion for one another.
 D. 2.2d—*Intent on one purpose.*
  i. Our purpose together is to advance the kingdom for the glory of God. We have a common vision.
  ii. Personal agendas have no place in the body.

IV. Philippians 2.3–4: Four Ways to Maintain Unity
 A. 2.3a—*Do nothing from selfish ambition.*
  i. Self-seeking leads to quarreling, haggling, fighting, arguing, and contending.
  ii. Galatians 5.20b–21a—it is a work of the flesh.
 B. 2.3b—Do nothing from *conceit.*
  i. A state of mind that seeks personal glory. An arrogant spirit.
  ii. An attitude of self-promotion must be removed.
 C. 2.3c—Be humble.
  i. Unity begins when we *count others more significant than ourselves.*

      ii. Humility described the mindset of a slave: "unfit, low, common."
        D. 2.4a—*Look not to your own interests, but rather to the interests of others.*
  i. Our aim is not just to take care of our own interests.
  ii. We must be involved in the lives of others. Their needs and concerns must surpass our own.

Reaction

1. As we focus on Philippians 1.27—2.4: what is Paul's primary focus? Unity in doctrine … or unity in attitude? Explain.

2. What does it mean to stand together? How does Paul explain it in Philippians 1.27b?

3. Why is it important to always remember the mission as we work together? When this occurs, what happens to all the internal issues inside a congregation?

4. How have your experiences with suffering united you with other brethren?

5. Why is a self-seeking person almost always in conflict with everyone else?

6. What is humility? How was this virtue looked upon in the first century world? What about our world today? Why is it a key characteristic of discipleship?

7. What are some ways you can find joy in making others joyful?

For Today's Christian

Unity comes when believers think alike. Self-seeking pursuits will be a problem that always confronts us. Envy and rivalry (Philippians 1.15) were the motive of those who afflicted Paul while he was imprisoned (Philippians 1.17). It is very easy for the selfish person to focus on the differences he or she has with others. They are almost always in conflict with others. In Corinth, Paul urged the brethren to be *united in the same mind and the same judgment*. This was the solution to their factions (1 Corinthians 1.10). Paul's exhortations on unity in Philippians and 1 Corinthians go far beyond doctrine. What he has in view is our attitude, mindset, and disposition inside the local congregation. We get there by:

- Romans 8.4–5—thinking in harmony with the Spirit.
- Romans 12.3—thinking with sober judgment.
- Romans 15.5—committing to live in harmony with one another.

Difficulty brings us together. In Philippians 1.28–30 Paul focuses on the difficulty he and the Philippian Christians faced. He says suffering is a gift of grace from God. That may challenge our human thinking just a little. But, when we suffer for the faith, it leads us toward our heavenly reward. It strengthens the church. And it wins the lost. A recent challenge for churches all over the globe was the response to the COVID-19 pandemic. Some applied the principles Paul speaks of in this section and survived. Others even thrived. Others, sadly, succumbed to division and discord. There may be more difficulties on the horizon. Will local congregations learn to apply Paul's teaching in Philippians 1.27-2.4 to be prepared for whatever comes?

Humility is a key characteristic of discipleship. Humility is where we count others as more significant than ourselves. It is very easy to think of ourselves more highly than we ought to think. For example, we often have little difficulty seeing the shortcomings and failures of others, while glossing over our own. We are usually very patient with our own failures and then begin to hold ourselves up on a higher plane than others. We can be less patient with others ... which leads to conflict. Problems of discord, division, and factionalism will end when we hold others as more worthy of respect and honor than ourselves.

Pray For ...

1. A deepening of the unity within your congregation, by strengthening your spiritual character, building a spirit of sharing and humility, empowering the proclamation of the gospel, and providing comfort and support during times of suffering.

2. An increased awareness of God's love and presence in your life, deepening your connection with fellow believers and inspiring a greater desire for unity, being motivated by Christ's love and compassion, and to be enabled to extend that love and mercy to others.

3. For help in thinking the same way, have the same love, be united in spirit, and be intent on one purpose, cultivating a humble attitude that values others, setting aside selfish ambitions and conceit, and genuinely caring for the interests of others.

Journal

As we move in our relationships, it is not about what others are or where they're at. The focus is, *will I count them as worthy of my help and encouragement? Will I serve my brother or sister? Will I take the time to do things that help build them up?* As you think about the work ahead, what are some ways you can make the good of others the focus of your life?

For Further Study

As Paul concludes this section on unity and working together, he points the readers mind to Jesus. He says, *adopt the same attitude as that of Christ Jesus,* 2.5. Read Philippians 2.6-8 and describe how Jesus did nothing from selfishness or conceit. How did he regard others as more important than Himself? In what ways did he set aside his own importance? Why did He come?

Endnotes

1. Scholar L. L. Welborn extensively documents the ancient political use of the same word for a "cleft in political consciousness" or "civil strife" and cites 1 Clement as a confirmation of this sense at Corinth. Clement asks the Corinthians, "Why are there quarrels and anger and dissension and divisions [*schismata*] and war among you?" (46:5). "The terms with which *schisma* is associated make it clear that it is neither a religious heresy nor a harmless clique that the author has in mind, but factions engaged in a struggle for power" (1987:87). See Johnson, Alan F. 1 Corinthians. Vol. 7 of *The IVP New Testament Commentary Series*. Westmont, IL: IVP Academic, 2004.
2. Schreiner, Thomas R. *1 Corinthians: An Introduction and Commentary.* Edited by Eckhard J. Schnabel. Vol. 7 of *Tyndale New Testament Commentaries.* London: Inter-Varsity Press, 2018, p. 263.
3. Shouse, Roger. "Jumpstart #3110." Jumpstarts Daily Devotional. Online. Charlestownroadcoc.org.
4. Um, Stephen T. *1 Corinthians: The Word of the Cross.* Edited by R. Kent Hughes. *Preaching the Word.* Wheaton, IL: Crossway, 2015, p. 221.
5. MacArthur, John F., Jr. *1 Corinthians. MacArthur New Testament Commentary.* Chicago: Moody Press, 1984, p. 319.
6. Um, p. 226.
7. MacArthur, p. 335.
8. Um, p. 230.
9. Um, p. 232.
10. MacArthur, p. 341.
11. Foulkes, Francis. *Ephesians: An Introduction and Commentary.* Vol. 10 of *Tyndale New Testament Commentaries.* Downers Grove, IL: InterVarsity Press, 1989, Vol. 10, p. 118.
12. Hughes, R. Kent. *Ephesians: The Mystery of the Body of Christ. Preaching the Word.* Wheaton, IL: Crossway Books, 1990, p. 124.
13. 1 Timothy 3.9; 4.1, 6; Titus 1.4.
14. Foukles, Vol. 10, p. 119.

www.ingramcontent.com/pod-product-compliance
Lightning Source LLC
Chambersburg PA
CBHW060845050426
42453CB00008B/842